Betrayed by the Justice System

What was done in the dark

will be brought into the light.

ROBIN SWAZIEK AND

DAVE SWAZIEK

ESTD   2021

Megan's
BOOKS

Betrayed by the Justice System

© 2021 by Robin Swaziek and Dave Swaziek

All rights reserved solely by the author. The author guarantees all contents are original and do not infringe upon the legal rights of any other person or work. No part of this book may be reproduced in any form without the permission of the author. The views expressed in this book are not necessarily those of the publisher.

Printed in the United States of America.

ISBN-13: 978-1-7369513-0-9

LCCN: 2021915285

Megan's Books

Loves Park, Illinois

DEDICATION

This book is dedicated to Megan by keeping her memory alive and her story never forgotten.

WE LOVE YOU MEGAN!

Acknowledgements

To our daughters Kristy and Melissa who have been with us through this nightmare all the time going through their own grief of losing their sister. You have been there for us every step supporting us standing with us for the fight for justice holding us up when we were falling. Megan loved you both as we do! Love, Mom and Dad.

To Megan's three beautiful kids Ethan, Kaeden and Robbie Marie always know you were your mom's most precious gifts. She loved all of you with all her heart. She lives on through each of you.

To our other grandkids Dylan, Kaitlyn and Kara, we love you and always remember "Aunt Mer" as Megan was lovingly called loved you with all of her heart, she adored being your aunt and she is with you always.

Last but not least, to our last granddaughter Olivia Megan who carries Megan's name even though "Aunt Mer" didn't get to meet you in person. Know that she loves you more than you will ever know she would be so honored to be your "Aunt Mer". We will make sure you know how special your "Aunt

Mer" is and know you have a special angel with you always. You all are a true blessing, and you make our darkest days brighter as we are honored to be your Nana and Baba. We love all of you from the bottom of our hearts.

To Nick who is now our son-in-law at the time of this nightmare you were so new to this family you and Melissa had not been dating very long when our family was changed forever. You were with us for all of it helping out being there for all of us especially Melissa taking care of her in her grief doing little things that meant so much to all of us always there for us with our technical issues. We are so glad this nightmare didn't push you away. Your love for Melissa obviously was strong even then we are so glad that you stuck with us through all of this and now our son-in-law.

To Bob – Kristy's fiancé – you also were with us helping in any way possible from the moment the call came during all the ugliness of planning a funeral you were there for whatever we needed. Thank You!

To Cindi Koroll, thank you for taking this case when so many others wouldn't even give us the time of day you saw the horrible injustice being done jumped right in and fought hard with us to get justice for Megan your passion your hard work will never be forgotten. You truly were Megan's Angel.

To family and friends for always supporting us, and for loving our Megan and the countless people who we didn't know that have reached out to us showing their outrage at the injustice that was done to Megan and our family in this criminal case. Thank You!

To every other victim of intoxicated drivers whose experienced injustice with our justice system. Laws need to be harder on people drinking and driving behind the wheel of anything that can take a life. These laws must be enforced no matter who you are and who you know if a life is taken there needs to be accountability and responsibility.

To Peter, Meg, and Katie - Thank You for your patience and encouragement with us during the writing of this book it wasn't an easy task, but the story needs to be told the justice system failed our daughter. We couldn't have done it without your help. Thank You!

Table of Contents

Chapter One

Becoming a Mom

I was raised in the sixties and seventies when life was so much simpler than it is today. There were no cell phones, no social media, and many of the modern-day distractions just did not exist. It was a slower paced time. The demanding schedules that we see young families striving to follow were not part of this era.

I am the oldest of four. I have two sisters and we are all two years apart. Then, when I was nine years old, a brother came along. We spent weekends camping, boating, riding bikes, and simply hanging out with family. It was like the kind of family you'd see on older TV shows. Sure, there were struggles that popped up here and there, but they were quickly forgotten because of the strong love within the household.

It was the ideal atmosphere for producing healthy confident children. Unfortunately, there were other circumstances molding the person I was which my parents had no knowledge of. Molestation at the hands of my grandfather was one of them. I did not understand at the time how this experience was molding and shaping me as a person or how it might affect my future. The shame and traumatic nature of the events kept me silent as it does with most victims of this kind of abuse. Unfortunately, the victim often turns the shame they feel from the event into insecurities. Maybe it was because of something I did. Maybe this is all I am worth.

My secret and the lies that accompanied it were like poison slowly dripping into my veins from an IV. There was no way I could have known or understood all the ways it was affecting my daily life back then or how it would dictate my future. It wasn't until I was 25 that this truth would be brought to light.

I had some very good friends in high school. We were close, and we had many good times, but I was always the quiet and shy one. I always went with the flow of my friend group but inside kind of felt like I was pretending to be happy. I can look back now and see the many insecurities I struggled with never thinking I could measure up to the expectations of others and never sure if I could truly trust them. It is not easy to 'be yourself' around others when you what you think of yourself falls short.

I suppose that is why, my best friends during this time were my cats and dogs. I loved them. They gave me unconditional love, and I always felt they really were there for me. With pets, you don't have to explain yourself or act a certain way. You don't have to pretend to be happy or be someone you are not. You can sit and be quiet and they seem to understand what you need.

When I was in high school not many girls went to college like they do today. I had no interest in going to college. What I really wanted was to get married and have babies. I wanted to become a mom. When I was a senior, I used to babysit for a family with two children. My family knew the family well. The mother of the children I babysat had a brother-in-law that was in the military and was coming home. She wanted to set us up on a date. He was four years older than me and had been away in the military. I was finishing high school and he had already experienced life as an adult not to mention life in the military. I could not imagine why he would want to go out with a high school senior but she convinced him to go out with me. She decided that her and her husband would come as well. I was very nervous to go out with someone who was not in high school. I wondered how we would relate to each other and what he thought about going on a date with a high school senior. He had his own place and was older than the guys I was used to being around. For our date, we went to dinner with his brother and his brother's wife, which was a good thing because both of us were very quiet so they broke the ice. We could rely on them to get the conversation started.

After our first date, he started picking me up from school. He worked the second shift and I got out of school at noon, so he would be there to take me home. Shortly after I met him, I got mono. I was pretty sick and missed a few weeks of school but to my surprise he would still come by my house before he went to work bringing me my favorite pop. He would just hang out with me until he had to leave for work. Needless to say, I was pretty taken with this guy and his kind actions. Shortly after I recovered from mono, it was time for my senior prom which he took me to. I could not believe a man who was in his twenties went to a high school prom because of his feelings for me. By this time I was sure he was the one for me.

I graduated high school shortly after prom, and I was spending as much time as possible with him. As our relationship progressed, we started talking about marriage. I was seventeen at the time of my graduation and we wanted to wait until I turned eighteen before we got married. We waited until two weeks after my eighteenth birthday. We were married in October. I moved in with him and tried to become a wife. I was young and I did my best to do the things I thought a wife should do. There are thousands of "how to be a wife" books on the market but never one tailored to your marriage specifically. I thought getting married would silence the demons of my childhood once and for all but instead it seemed to awaken them. Despite the many unknowns, I was still looking forward to starting this new season of my life.

My new husband worked second shift so I was alone a lot of the time and ended up growing lonely. It was a big change from high school student to wife. After six months of marriage, I said I would like to have a baby. I thought this would help with the loneliness. He agreed and in no time, I became pregnant. I was so happy that I was going to have my own baby, my own child to love and take care of.

I wanted a girl so bad but was sure I was having a boy. Back then, we did not have the luxury of ultrasound pictures telling us if we were having a boy or a girl. Expectant parents had no idea what sex the baby was until the moment the baby arrived. My daughter, my first baby, Kristy Lynn was born January 4th on a cold Saturday evening. On that day, my whole world changed for the better. I felt so much love for this brand new life. I had never felt this way before. All I wanted to do was hold her and protect her from all the harm in the world. I had given birth to a baby. I had become a mom and at that moment, I was the happiest I had ever been in my whole life. We went home in a couple days and I began my life as a Mom. Mom… the best title ever.

She was a good baby. I dressed her up all the time in beautiful outfits. I was very overprotective of her, as I did not want any harm to come to her. I would be her protector. Keeping her safe from all the things I had endured as a child. All the pains no one ever knew had happened in secret.

Life went on and we bought a house when Kristy was around two years old. I loved seeing her playing in the nice yard. She got her first swing set. I loved being her Mom and it seemed like all the boxes were being checked off. I had gotten married, I had a baby, we bought a house, and I was raising my daughter with all the love in my heart. Her Dad was working a lot of hours and at times I felt like it was just me and my little girl, but I loved being with her and watching her grow. After a few years, things between her Dad and me began falling apart.

The secret from my childhood was showing its ugly face within my marriage. When love and sex are tainted by things like I'd experienced and those past experiences are buried instead of pulled from the root and exposed, it becomes a breeding ground for marital issues. The old feeling that something was wrong with me visited me often. The feeling that I was not good enough was right under the surface, but I had no idea what these feelings were. I could not even put them into words and I did not know how to deal with them so I ran as fast as I could from those demons but not from my little girl. I loved her with all my heart and still tried to be the best mom I could. She was an adorable, active, beautiful little girl.

Her Dad and I divorced when she was 3 years old. Though it was rough, I will never regret marrying him because if I had not, I would not have had my first little girl who to this day is the best thing that ever happened to me. Kristy Lynn made me a Mom, a title I still think to this day is the best title I could ever hope for. Today Kristy Lynn is a Mom herself to three beautiful children. She has one boy and two girls who gave me the next best title of NANA. She is a wonderful Mom to her children; she is a caring, loving person and I am so proud to be her Mom.

When Kristy was around two, I took a part time job at an insurance company doing clerical work. After the divorce, I was promoted and started working full time. I had gone straight from my parent's home to being a wife at the age of eighteen to being a divorced, single mom a few years later. I can say that I was pretty much on a destructive path after the divorce. I had no idea where my life was headed at only 23 years old. I thought I had it all figured out five short years ago when I married right out of high school. But now, I was divorced, a single Mom, hurt, confused, and discouraged by the myth of living happily ever after. I felt all alone on the path of life. So, what was next? I realized I had nothing figured out.

However, the fact remained that I had always wanted to be a Mom, and I was thrilled to have my adorable little girl. She was still the best thing that had ever happened to me, so now I just had to figure out where we were going from here with our changed lives.

For the first few months after the divorce, I would go out with coworkers a couple times a week trying to fill the void I felt from no longer being a wife. I was single and trying to have a good time while not truly dealing with this new strange life that I found myself in. I would have my parents pick up Kristy from daycare and I would go out after work for hours. I would then pick Kristy up and go home again, thinking I was dealing with my new life and had everything under control. I had a pretty strict childhood growing up so I felt that this was my time to enjoy myself, knowing in the back of my mind I was just doing it to avoid confronting my emotions. I knew this was not the path for my child or me.

Chapter 2

Along Came David

Then one day at the office, a new person named David was transferred to our office from the safety department. He was single, easygoing, fun, and everyone instantly liked him. His desk was only a couple desks behind where I sat so I could hear him interacting with the other employees. I would hear him laughing and hear his easygoing manner. I think the thing that first attracted me to him was how he seemed to have it all together. He was never down and always seemed happy.

In many ways, he was the opposite of me during that time. I felt uneasy. I forced myself to act like everything was okay. I forced myself to act like nothing was wrong with me although I knew better deep down in my heart. I could feel in my gut that I was not in a good place, but I hadn't connected with those feelings yet. I hadn't talked about them with anyone or even allowed myself to go there. David soon started going out with us after work. He was easy to talk to, fun to be around, and eventually we decided to go out, just the two of us. We seemed to get along, enjoying each other's company and before we knew it, we were spending more and more time together.

It was scary. I wasn't sure I wanted to get involved in a relationship again after a failed marriage, and he was pretty focused on his career. Eventually I started including Kristy in our relationship. He took me to his family's farm three hours away to meet his family. I knew my feelings were getting more serious but I was still scared. I didn't want another disappointing failure. He was getting cold feet as well. After all, I was a package deal. I had a daughter and he wanted to move up the ladder at work. One night after discussing our feelings, we decided to step our relationship back. Right after that talk, I had such mixed emotions. Part of me thought it was probably for the best. It was definitely less scary than letting someone get close again but, I already missed the easygoing person I enjoyed being with. Something about him made me feel safe. His easygoing manner was contagious; I was in awe of it wishing I could be just a little bit like him.

David was raised on a dairy farm in Wisconsin in a very small town, the second of four children. He worked hard on the farm, went to school, and was very involved in sports. He wasn't raised with any demons or secrets to keep like I was. Something about that appealed to me even though at this time I was still convinced I had left my demons and secrets behind when I left my childhood home. Our talk about stepping back from each other only lasted a few hours. He called, and we talked some more and both decided we didn't like the idea. Not long after, he was in one of his childhood friend's wedding. He was going back to his small town and asked me to go along for the weekend. I was thrilled and was beginning to feel like we were a true couple. When we got home from the weekend, despite our earlier reservations on progressing our relationship, we just fell into being a couple.

The future started sneaking into our conversations. I was scared and excited, but also in love. Not long after that he asked me to marry him and I said yes. David had never been married before and wanted a wedding. On May 31, 1980, with Kristy as our flower girl, we were married in a beautiful church wedding. Kristy was five years old by this time.

We had talked about kids before we were married and we were both excited about expanding our family as quickly as possible. We both wanted more children. I was thrilled. This was a second chance to make my dreams come true. I had married this funny, caring man who loved me. He wanted to take care of me and my daughter *and* wanted more children. The world was right again.

We were both still working at the insurance company and adjusting to being a family. Kristy was always saying she wanted a sister and I was more than ready to have another baby. I was so ready for this next chapter of my life to begin. Dave was really good and extremely patient with Kristy as we all adjusted to this new life. I knew he would be a good Dad. He loved Kristy right away. Eight months after we were, married, Dave got a nice promotion but it involved moving 90 miles away from my hometown. I had never lived away from home. I was terrified but we packed up and started a new adventure.

We settled into a new town, a new home, and began hoping every month that I would become pregnant. I had to quit my job to move and Kristy was in first grade so she was gone all day. I didn't know anybody, Dave was busy with his new promotion, and I was feeling pretty lonely. We went back to my hometown to visit my family a lot on the weekends. Eventually I started meeting people and we moved into a nice subdivision with Kristy's school at the end of the street. We made some friends, joined a bowling league, had some great neighbors, and life went on. The only thing that wasn't happening was getting pregnant. I had not wanted so many years between my children.

Before I knew it, we were celebrating our third wedding anniversary. Kristy was now eight years old, and I was happy with our life except the void of another child. When I decided to have Kristy, I got pregnant right away. I was devastated over not being able to get pregnant again. Then in October of 1983, I knew I was pregnant. Sounds crazy but I just knew it finally had happened. I was so excited but wanted to wait until it was confirmed before shouting it to everyone.

We were going to have a baby. It was all we could think about. Finally, a baby would be added to our little family. They told me my due date was June 29, 1984 but I had done some research and counted the number of days. I came up with the due date of July 4, 1984. I started counting the days until July. Kristy was going to be nine and a half by the time this baby arrived so it would be like starting over. I didn't really have too many baby items left from when Kristy was a baby. After all this time, it was exciting getting ready for the new baby.

I started getting a nursery ready and planning for a newborn. Dave had never been around a baby much before but he was just as excited as I was for this baby's arrival. Kristy was excited also, but she had been an only child for so long, not having to share our attention that I was a little concerned. I didn't want her to feel left out. But she was such a good little girl. I knew she would be a great big sister. The pregnancy was fairly easy, but it was different from my first pregnancy. Dave and I went to classes that were never even talked about when I was pregnant with Kristy. It felt like dads could be so much more involved this time around. Dave would even be allowed in the delivery room with me. I counted down every day waiting for this baby. I was going to be a Mom again and could not have been more thrilled. June came and went with no baby but I wasn't worried because I was sure it was going to be a little fourth of July baby.

Tuesday, July 3rd came and I was feeling ready for this baby. I wanted the pregnancy to be over and wanted to hold my baby. Dave came home from work that day and we went out to dinner. Dave played basketball at our church on Tuesday nights with some guys including our neighbor. That night, when basketball was over, the neighbor and his wife came over to play cards. I had started feeling some discomfort in my back but didn't think too much about it. I had a curved spine so discomfort in my back was nothing new, even though it was a little more intense. I didn't say anything and the four of us started playing cards. About an hour into playing cards, I started feeling contractions. I still wasn't sure if I was in labor or not so I just kept playing cards. Then the contractions got where they stopped me in my tracks.

We decided it was time to head to the hospital. Kristy went home with our neighbors, and we headed to the hospital. We arrived there around 10:00 p.m. I was in labor and our baby was on the way. I was admitted, examined, and was told I had a ways to go and that it would definitely be after midnight before the baby came. Like I said earlier, it had been nine and a half years since I had delivered a baby but things seemed to be getting really intense with pain. The contractions were harder and then I knew it was time to push. We called the nurse into the room. She acted annoyed and had not even called the doctor yet but with my insistence, she finally examined me again and she started yelling to call the doctor. Dave was told to get his scrubs on, because baby was going to be here soon. The doctor arrived just in time to deliver our little girl. He didn't even have time to put scrubs on and ended up delivering her in his street clothes. Megan Marie was born on July 3rd, at 11:37 p.m. and we were over the moon with our little firecracker.

Chapter 3

Megan in the Middle

We brought Megan home two days after she was born, and we were so in love with this little human that we had waited so long for. Kristy was thrilled to have a sister and to help take care of her. Dave was a very hands-on Dad. He took a little time off work and we tried to get into a schedule as a tired, but excited family of four. Megan was a bald little thing. She would not take a bottle unless she had her right hand on her head. Later, when she finally got hair, she would always twirl it and did so into adulthood especially if she was bored, upset, or nervous. When she was little, my Dad used to tell her all the time that he was going to break her of that habit but, of course, he never did.

Soon after birth, Megan began to have an issue with eating. She would drink her bottle super-fast and it would all come back up. She didn't just spit up, we called them "gushers". She started to lose weight. Doctor said we needed to try a pacifier. The thought was that it would slow her down when she was getting a bottle. I was a little skeptical and didn't like the idea of a pacifier, but we tried the suggestion and it worked! She still had "gushers" but not as severe, and she started gaining weight again.

Sleep was another issue! For the first six weeks of her life, Megan wanted to sleep from late afternoon to early evening, wake up, go back to sleep around 10:00 p.m., wake up around 1:00 a.m., and then be back awake for hours. She pretty much wanted to be in her swing during this time. This was before motorized swings so her swing had to be hand cranked every ten minutes. The swing was by our bed and I would crank it every ten minutes for hours so she would be happy. We would try everything to wake her up and keep her awake earlier in the evening, but nothing worked. We were very happy when she was around six weeks and things changed. She would take her last bottle around 10:00 pm and sleep until five or six in the morning. First night she slept like that, I remember waking up in a panic because she didn't get me up as usual. I ran to her bed to check on her and she was very peacefully sleeping like an angel. She was a good baby, and we were so happy with our little family. She was our blonde haired, blue-eyed precious little girl who we adored.

Megan started walking at around thirteen months old. She would get excited at the sight of all of us. When she was old enough to realize that Kristy would leave for the day to go to school, I'd let her know when it was getting time for Kristy to come home and she'd go to the door and wait for her big sister to come home. She would get so excited when she saw Kristy coming. She also loved Scooby-Doo and wanted to watch it all the time. She would get upset if it wasn't on so I had to start taping the episodes just so she could watch it all the time. We had a few VCR tapes full of episodes just for her. Megan's love of Scooby-Doo was a constant thing for her even as a teenager. Her whole room was decorated with Scooby-Doo and even her first car had many Scooby-Doo accessories added to it.

When Megan was born, I wasn't working. I loved being home with her all day as a full-time mom. It was where I always wanted to be, a mom to two beautiful girls. When Megan was around eighteen months old, she started getting ear infections all the time. She would be sick, run a temperature, and wouldn't eat. I was always running her to the doctor. She started being on antibiotics a lot. After a few months, the doctor started talking about putting tubes in her ears.

Around the same time, Dave received another big promotion, which would involve a lot of overnight traveling. I said I wanted to move back to my hometown then, to be closer to my family if he was going to be gone overnight a lot. He could travel just as easily from there.

Doctors were still talking about tubes for Megan's ears, but I told them I was going to wait until we moved back. I would find a doctor and discuss options after the move. The promotion and the move happened rather quickly. By this time, we had been gone from my hometown for almost six years. We found a house to rent while we decided where we wanted to buy. We moved home a week before Megan's second birthday. It was a whirlwind few months. The promotion, deciding to move home, finding a place to live, packing and moving in approximately six weeks with two girls was a lot, but we did it. We got settled in and celebrated Megan's birthday with more family attending because we were home. It was good to be back.

Megan started getting strep throat at least twice a month now. It moved from her ears to her throat. She would be so sick, run a 104 fever, throw up, and be lethargic for days. She was on antibiotics more than she was off. It was a hard thing to watch. She wouldn't eat and so she was small for her age. All the medicines she was on combined with not being able to eat well had stunted her growth.

Shortly after moving home, we started talking about having another baby. Megan was two and we knew we wanted another child. I thought three years between them was a nice age gap. Megan, when not sick, was such a good, caring little girl. She loved animals, loved being outside, and she became friends with her cousins who now lived close by. She went to see my parents so much more and enjoyed being with them. I started watching my nephew Kevin who was fifteen months older than Megan, My sister, his mom, was a single mom who worked a lot of hours to support him. I wasn't working so I was more than happy to have him. The bond between him and Megan grew very strong in a very short period of time.

We started looking for a house to buy in the school district where I grew up still hoping every month that I would get pregnant again. After looking for a while, we were shown a brand new subdivision being developed so we decided to build a house and picked out a lot where we wanted to build. About the same time we made the decision to build, I found out I was pregnant with our third child. I say "our" third child because Dave had never tried to replace Kristy's Dad, but he loved her as his own. We were excitedly expecting baby number three.

It was a crazy time in our lives. Kristy was a teenager, Megan was three and still sick a lot, I was pregnant, and we were building a house. We moved into our new house at the end of May 1988, six weeks before Megan's fourth birthday. I was seven months pregnant and exhausted. I was having issues with the pregnancy and was miserable. My July due date came and went and my doctor started doing stress tests every other day on the baby. I had high blood pressure and toxemia so the doctor put me on bed rest, hoping I would go into labor on my own. He thought if I went into labor, I would have another fast, easy delivery, so we waited.

Friday, August 12th came. I had a doctor's appointment in the morning and there was still no progress. He told me to go home, make arrangements for the girls, and meet him at the hospital Monday morning. They would have to take our baby. I was ready. I was two weeks overdue. I went home feeling discouraged. I did not want a C-section. My Mom had come over for dinner that night and we were playing a game when I felt contractions, was I imaging it? No, they were real!! Luckily, my Mom was there to stay with Megan, because once they started they were coming fast and hard. We arrived at the hospital around 10:00 p.m.. The baby had the cord wrapped around her neck twice, and it was a tough delivery but at 11:11 p.m. on August 12th,1988 our third little girl was born. Melissa Ann completed our family. I was exhausted but again so in love with this little human who had been so stubborn to come into the world.

We were a family of five with three girls and I was so happy. We had our new baby and a new house. Dave started traveling more with his new promotion, and I became a full time Mom to a thirteen year old, a four year old, and a newborn. We settled into this new chapter. Both Kristy and Megan loved the new baby. Megan was always trying to help feed and change her. Kristy was a busy, active teenager by now. She was busy with friends and all that comes with being a teenager but she loved her little sisters.

I was still watching my nephew a lot and as Melissa got older, the bond between the three of them grew. They looked at him as a brother. We went to Dave's folk's farm a lot. My nephew went with us often as his Mom was still working many hours. They were a trio. We would go to the farm and the kids would experience what seemed like a different world. There were baby cows, barns, tractors, fields, and acres to explore. They always had a great time and were worn out when it was time to come home. The Swaziek farm became one of Megan's favorite places even as an adult. It had been in the family since the 1800's and was always a beautiful place to go.

One time when we were at the farm, we went to a Wal-Mart in a nearby town. Melissa was still very young, Megan was five, and Kevin was six. They spotted these adorable pink and blue bears that were $5.00 each. Megan and Kevin wanted one. Megan of course got a pink one and Kevin got a blue one, and instantly Megan was calling hers "pink bear" and Kevin's was "blue bear." Those were their names from that moment on. It was the best $10.00 I ever spent. They played with those bears every day. They would have the bears get married, go to the farm, play babies, and sleep with them. Megan remained attached to "pink bear" even into adulthood. I had washed it so many times; it was kind of a grayish pink after all the washings and years.

Once, one of our dogs had gotten a hold of it and chewed part of "pink bear's" nose off. Megan was so upset and mad at that dog but that was the last time pink bear wasn't put up safely if she wasn't home. Megan slept with it and cried with it if she was upset about something. It went everywhere she did. She always said, even as a teenager, that "pink bear" would be in her bouquet when she got married, and that she wanted to be buried with "pink bear." That $5.00 bear became Megan's best confident forever. It didn't make it into her wedding bouquet because by the time she got married she wasn't a huge fan of flowers so she had a fairly small bouquet but "pink bear" did go to Mexico with her on her honeymoon. I thought she was kidding but after they got to their hotel and checked in, she sent me a picture of "pink bear" on their bed in their hotel room. I just smile and still do every time I think of that or whenever I come across that picture. She was 29 when she got married but age did not matter when it came to going out of the country, "pink bear" went along with her. "Pink bear" was always on her bed.

As they got older, Megan, Kevin, and Melissa were together all the time. We spent summer days at the local pool with neighbors and friends. Before I knew it, Megan and Melissa were in school and Kristy was almost out of school. Melissa was very involved in traveling basketball. We would spend the weekends with the families of the girls that were on Melissa's team and, of course, Megan went along. She kept score and cheered her sister and the other girls on. We usually were there for the weekend so we would all stay in a hotel, and Megan made sure she looked out for all those girls while we were there. She was very protective of them.

The years went by fast, too fast. Dave was traveling a lot. He would call home every night to talk with the girls before bedtime. Megan was still sick a lot with strep. One year, she missed as much school as she was there. Her doctor kept saying she would outgrow it and I believed him but I watched Megan get sick so much. When I would talk to the doctor, he just acted like I was overreacting.

We hosted big family get-togethers at the holidays. My sister and Kevin, along with my parents, would spend the night on Christmas Eve even though they only lived a few miles away. We wanted the girls and Kevin together so they could experience the joy of Santa coming on Christmas morning. Both Megan and Melissa adored Kevin. He was more like a brother to them than a cousin. My parents just wanted to be there to watch the magic of Christmas with the kids. Later in the day, my sisters, their kids, and my brother would join us for a big meal, gift giving, and enjoying the day together. It was always a magical day.

Even though Kristy was out of school, she still adored her little sisters and was very involved in their lives. I was involved in school outings and helped out in their classrooms when they were in grade school. I loved being a full time, hands on Mom to my girls. On the weekends or the days that Dave wasn't traveling, we enjoyed being a family and doing things that families do. The girls adored their Dad; they had him wrapped around their little fingers. We were a close family, and involved in everything in their lives. They were spoiled somewhat but so loved and cherished. They were good girls. We were so proud of them and I was never ashamed to take them anywhere. They were well behaved and got along well. I was always enjoyed dressing them up and taking lots of pictures which I especially cherish now.

Chapter 4

The Difficult Road

By the time Megan was in sixth grade, she was still sick a lot. The usual antibiotics were not working anymore, as her body was immune to them, so they kept putting her on stronger meds. It was so hard to watch her so sick, but I kept believing her pediatrician that she would outgrow this. By this time, I had a good friend that was a pediatric nurse. She finally told me to stop believing this pediatrician and insist on a referral to a specialist, as I should have done years ago, so I did. The doctor still thought I was an overreacting mom, but I held my ground. I was so tired of watching Megan so sick and missing many special moments because she was running a fever of 104, throwing up, and just plain miserable. I took her to the specialist. He took one look at her files and said her tonsils and adenoids needed to come out as soon as possible. Her tonsils were so bad. He said she never would outgrow this since her tonsils were just too diseased. We scheduled the surgery right away. I was so torn. I didn't want to see Megan have surgery but if this would really help, I sure wanted to see her better. I put my trust in this doctor, hoping he was right. The surgery was supposed to be a six-hour outpatient procedure but she ended up being admitted and was there for two days.

When the Doctor went to remove her tonsils, they were adult size and so diseased they kept breaking into pieces. The incisions were so deep and she woke up throwing up and in so much pain. I felt like the worst mom because I believed her pediatrician when he said she would outgrow this instead of listening to my inner feelings. I was so upset and mad at myself, beating myself up over and over all night while I watched her laying in that hospital bed looking so miserable. The next morning her pediatrician stuck his head in the door of her hospital room saying, "oh I hear she had a rough time with the removal of her tonsils." I was tired, upset, and furious with this man. I just glared at him saying nothing, not trusting what would come out if I opened my mouth. He just turned away looking smug and left. Needless to say, my girls never stepped foot in his office again. I immediately found a new pediatrician.

We took Megan home and slowly started the long road to recovery. We had done this over Christmas break hoping she wouldn't miss a lot of school but that didn't work. The incisions from the removal of her tonsils were so deep that even when she started to feel a little better and got hungry, it was too painful for her to swallow. She would cry and wouldn't eat. It was pure torture to watch her go through this. We would try all kinds of different things for her to eat. My parents and different family members would bring her ice cream, popsicles and milkshakes. It was a rough six weeks before she was finally on the mend and able to swallow without a lot of pain.

Megan had insisted before surgery that she wanted to keep her tonsils after they were removed. I made sure, asking numerous times for them to come home with us. She wanted to take those diseased tonsils to school for show and tell and she did. When she was fully recovered from this horrible ordeal, she was on an antibiotic just once during the rest of her childhood. Thank God for the knowledge of the specialist. She was always smaller than the rest of the family because of all the medication she was on in the early part of her life. We are all on the tall side. Kristy and I are the shortest of the five of us at 5'8". Megan was 5'3" and barely 100 pounds when she graduated. Later on in life, she would wear three to four inch heels so she wouldn't look so much shorter than all of us when we took family pictures. She was small but she was feisty. Megan had an awesome close relationship with many great friends as she entered junior high and high school. So many of these relationships carried on into adulthood.

Megan had a special bond with my Dad who was known lovingly as "Papa". He was a kid at heart and enjoyed being around his grandkids. She loved tomatoes and my Dad would plant her own tomato plant in his garden with a sign that said "Megan's Tomatoes" and no one had better take a tomato from that plant. When she was twelve, my Dad had a freak accident. He fell and hit his head and laid in a coma with head trauma for twelve days before he was pronounced brain dead. It was an awful time in our lives. He had always made everyone laugh and all the grandkids adored him. The last picture I have of my Dad was taken just a few weeks before his accident. It was taken at our house during a family get together. The picture is of him and Megan on the trampoline. He wanted Megan to show him how to do the flips she was doing. Now, my Dad was a big guy and Megan was just a little thing especially on that trampoline next to him. It was the funniest thing. I grabbed my camera trying to take pictures of this priceless memory while all the time laughing so hard that I was sure none of them would turn out. Those were the days before digital cameras. After his death, when I finally got around to developing that roll of film, I was amazed at how good the pictures turned out. My Dad "Papa" and Megan having the time of their lives on that trampoline. Priceless!!

Within a year of Papa's death, we lost another very close family member and Megan lost a couple of school friends due to accidents. It was a rough time for her. She was depressed for quite a while and kept it all to herself and probably "pink bear".

I was caught up in my own grief at losing my Dad. He was only 62 and his death was so unexpected. Megan knew I was hurting so she didn't say much to me for a while. When I finally realized she was in a bad place and suggested she get into some grief counseling, she opened up a little to me and said she didn't want to say anything to me because she knew how sad I was from losing "Papa". She didn't want to make me feel worse. She was concerned about me and my loss. We both tried dealing with our loss and life went on.

Megan was in high school by now and had a great circle of friends. She was funny, witty, and had a smile that would light up a room as I was told over and over again. She would do things around the house like turn my framed pictures on the wall upside down or mix up the pictures of the girls, which I had in age order, just to see how long it would take me to notice. I loved my clocks that made music or chimed. She would call them "noise makers". I would realize the clocks were quiet, thinking maybe the batteries were dead. But more than once the batteries were gone due to Megan. This even continued when she was an adult. She would get the biggest kick out of doing these things. It was all in fun and I smile just thinking of these moments now.

Even though Melissa was bigger and taller than Megan, Megan let her know she was her younger sister and would look out for her. As the two of them got older, their bond was so much more than sisters, they were best friends. That bond only grew stronger as the years went on even into adulthood. It was them against the world. They went to each other for everything. Megan was a good student and was on the swim team in high school until one of her friends who was also on the swim team died in a horrible accident, Megan wouldn't go back. She said it was too hard without her friend there. She was helpful around the house and loved our family dogs with a passion. She graduated high school and we were very proud parents of the young woman she had become. We were so thankful for our little firecracker and excited to see what the future held for her. If we only knew what that future would entail and the horrible heartache, we would go through because of one person's irresponsible actions.

Chapter 5

The Day on the River

As my girls grew up and became adults, I became a mom with a full heart. Blessed to be the mother of three beautiful daughters. The best thing in my life. The best joy I've ever experienced. There is no feeling like it in the world. All my girls were wanted, loved, and perfect in every way. But on June 24, 2016, nine days before Megan's 32nd birthday, I also became a mother with a gaping hole in my heart. This was the day our worst nightmare began.

That Friday started out, I guess, like most days. We headed to work with the thought that the weekend was only a few hours away. My little dog had a bad accident in May where her front leg was broken. It was an open break so she was in surgery for hours. She had screws and pins put in so I had to take her to the vet a couple times a week for check-ups. It had been a long month, a nightmare in my mind, but she was doing so much better. The vet was sure she was going to have full use of her leg again, so that Friday morning I was feeling like there was light at the end of this nightmare. I did not realize that by the end of this day I would really know what it was to be in a true, horrible nightmare with no light at the end.

I had an appointment when I got off work at the vet for another checkup and treatment. Dave wanted to go visit his mom who lives in a nursing home five hours away. Since I had to go to the vet, we decided he would go up Friday morning and come back Saturday. I went to the vet appointment and then had dinner with my sister. We ate dinner, sat, and talked for a while then said our goodbyes and headed home. It was close to 9:00 p.m. I know this because I pulled into a dollar store to get some allergy pills when I realized they were closing so I just headed on home. A few minutes later my phone rang. I glanced at it and saw it was my sister in law but I was driving so decided not to answer and call her back when I got home. I was only about ten minutes away. I did not know that in just a few minutes my life was going to change forever.

I drove a little further and was stopped at a red light when my phone rang again. I looked at it and saw it was my sister this time. I wondered why she was calling since I just left her. My only thought was something was wrong with our mother who has medical issues. I was still sitting there so I answered it and could tell right away by her voice that something was wrong.

She asked where I was. I told her I was at a stop light a few minutes from home. I asked her again what was wrong. By this time, the light had turned green but I was not hanging up until I found out what was going on. She finally said that Megan had been in a bad accident. She told me they were doing CPR on her and she was headed to the hospital in an ambulance. My sister told me she was in my driveway waiting for me. I was only a few minutes from home but I don't remember the drive home from that moment on. Then Dave called upset asking what was going on with Megan because he had also received a call saying she had been in an accident. He was on his way home. I told him all I knew was Megan had been in an accident, was receiving CPR, and was in route to the hospital. I had no idea which hospital as we have three hospitals in town and the accident happened approximately 45 minutes away.

By this time, I was home, my sister was in the driveway upset, and I probably yelled at her asking where Megan was headed. She said she had called all three hospitals and they knew nothing about an accident victim coming. At this point, all I remember was yelling and screaming in my driveway. I am sure cursing and yelling, "What are we going to do?" I think my sister received a call from our sister-in-law saying where Megan was being taken. I just remember her saying to get in her car and we were heading to the hospital. I was crying and shaking so bad but at that moment, I knew Megan was gone. I tried to call Kristy and Melissa because I knew they had to come to the hospital. I said to my sister, "She is gone. Megan is gone." My sister said, "Don't say that. She's just been in an accident."

But I knew. I knew my child was gone. I tried calling Megan's husband but couldn't even finish the call. My sister had to finish talking to him. I felt so physically sick. My Megan, my beautiful daughter, was gone. I knew it.

By this time, we were pulling into the parking lot of the hospital. Dave called wanting to know what was going on. I told him we had just gotten to the hospital at the same time as an ambulance was backing up to the ER doors. I knew Megan was in there. I just remember getting out of the car and running that way as a couple paramedics were coming out of the hospital with an empty gurney. They said they had brought the young lady from the boating crash in, but of course, I had to go into the ER. Within seconds a nurse came out asking if I knew the young woman that just came in, asking who I was, what was her name? I answered her questions just wanting to see my daughter and wanting to know what happened. She left me and my sister sitting there and in no time at all a nurse and a doctor came walking towards us. I knew what they were going to say but did not want to hear the words. I felt terror inside. I felt like I was screaming, "NO!" but I don't know if the word actually came out of my mouth.

The doctor was in front of me at this time informing me of what I already knew. Megan was gone. He said in a matter of fact tone that her injuries were so severe that she could not have survived. I was crying. I felt like I was going to throw up. How was this possible? She had just texted me hours before. This is when my world changed forever. One of my girls was gone. I could not even wrap my head around the words. My whole body felt limp. The memories of the rest of the night come in pieces. I am not even sure of what happened when.

I wanted to see Megan. They tried to prepare me as to what I would see; what kind of shape Megan was in. As I started walking back to the room where she was, I thought I was going to faint. My legs felt rubbery. I felt like I was shaking inside and out. I felt physically sick trying to prepare for what I would see as I entered the room where she was. She was lying there. My beautiful daughter. There was a brace around her neck, a tube down her throat, bruising, scrapes, and her beautiful hair around her face. Her eyes were closed. I went to her, crying and grabbing her hand just wanting her to wake up. "Wake up, Megan!!"

After going back and seeing Megan, they put me and my sister in a room where in no time Kristy, Melissa, and other family members started showing up. As soon as they saw me, they knew Megan was gone. I remember sitting in the room surrounded by people who loved Megan and were in the same disbelief as I was. Everyone was crying. I had my head in a garbage can throwing up as my oldest grandson held my hair back, taking care of me, and answering my phone as Dave called. He knew Megan was gone and was stuck on some highway trying to get back to us.

At some point, a woman from the coroner's office showed up and started talking to me informing me they were going to take Megan down to the morgue. I told her no because her Dad was driving back from up north. He needed to see Megan. Her phone rang and she said she needed to take the call. She came back saying that the call was from the sheriff in the town where the crash happened and she began to tell me the details which lead us to this moment.

There had been a boating crash. Megan was on my brother's pontoon boat. She loved boating. My Dad had always had a boat and my girls were on a pontoon boat before they could even walk. Dad would call and we would go out on the boat for the day. When the girls were little, I would take their strollers and we would go. We loved it. My brother had the love of boating also. He had a boat that he kept at a campground and that is where Megan was spending her Friday night, doing what she loved, going for a pontoon ride with her uncle.

They got on the boat with another couple and were going to watch the sunset. From my understanding and the reports, they had not been on the boat very long. They were just idling, waiting for the sunset when they saw and heard a jon boat roaring towards them. Assuming the jon boat was going to turn, I guess they watched for a second, then realized it wasn't turning. People on the pontoon started standing and waving and honking the horn. My brother decided he was going to get out of the way so he put his boat in gear and turned the boat but the jon boat hit the pontoon going up onto the back deck striking Megan as she was sitting in the back; her favorite place to sit. The jon boat hit Megan in her chest throwing her into the river. I have listened to the video statements from that night and still can only imagine the terror as the crash happened.

The driver of the jon boat was intoxicated. He admitted he never even saw the pontoon boat. At the time of the crash, it was completely light out. It was approximately 8:30 on a summer night and was not dark out at all. How do you not see a pontoon boat? I was told at the hospital that the person who hit Megan had been arrested for an OUI (operating under influence) and reckless endangerment. I asked if he was in jail and was told yes.

After hearing the details, I was told they needed to take Megan down to the morgue, and it was time for anyone who wanted to go back and see her to say goodbye. I said, "You cannot take her until her Dad gets here. He's driving from up north and wants to see her. You cannot take her!" She said that when he got back we could come down to the morgue to see Megan.

I watched in disbelief as loved ones went back to see Megan and would return crying. I wanted to wake up from this nightmare! This could not be happening! Finally, I was asked if I wanted to go back before they took Megan to the morgue. I needed to be with my daughter alone. My sisters, one on each side of me, took me back. I felt like I couldn't even walk. I felt like they carried me back to the room where my daughter laid. I wanted to be alone with Megan so my sisters waited in the hall as I went in to be with my daughter. I sat next to the bed holding her hand and twirling her hair, a habit she had done her whole life. She always twirled her hair. I remembered how soft her hair felt as I sat there twirling it, crying, and begging her to open her eyes. I am not sure how long I sat there just being with her, just the two of us. Finally, my sisters came in and said it was time to go. I did not want to leave her. I wanted her to wake up and tell me about her boo boo this time. Megan was always coming home saying, "Mom, I got a boo boo."

They kept saying it was time. They had to take her. I got up and felt like my knees were going to buckle. I did not want to leave my girl there alone. I was screaming inside, "NO!! Please, someone do something! Make her wake up!"

It felt like my sisters did my walking for me as we went back out to the waiting room where everyone was. They sat me in a chair. Dave had called asking if I was going to wait at the hospital. He was still two hours away. It was 12:30 am. They were going to take Megan at any time to the morgue so I wanted to go home. He said he would meet me there.

My sister went to get the car. Again, I tried to stand up feeling as if my knees were going to buckle. My legs did not want to work. My 17-year-old grandson, who had been by my side since he got there, held onto me, and helped me to the car. My sister took me back home where both my sisters, my girls, my nieces, and my grandson all waited with me until Dave got there. I do not really remember the next couple of hours at home. I know I had a keychain with all three of the girls' pictures on it and I just held it, sometimes crying, just in shock and disbelief.

Dave finally got there around 2:30 in the morning. He came in the front door. We were all downstairs in the family room, quiet except the sounds of sobbing at times. He called me upstairs into the kitchen. We went out to the deck and just cried and hugged each other. After a few minutes, Kristy and Melissa came out and the four of us just hung on to each other crying, in such shock. How was this possible? We were missing a big piece of our family. Dave wanted to go see Megan so everyone started to leave.

I am so thankful for my family that never left me alone. I am sure I did not say thank you to them but I am so thankful for them. We got into Kristy's SUV and left around 3:00 in the morning for the morgue. This could not be real! This could not be happening!! We got downtown to the morgue and called them to let us in at this crazy hour. She said she would take us to a room, and we could see Megan through a window. Dave said no. He wanted to kiss her goodbye. After some talking, we were able to actually be in the same room as Megan. Again, so many feelings, tears, and disbelief overtook us. This could not be happening. We finally left and it was so difficult to leave Megan there. We were still in such shock over everything. How could Megan be gone? We brought her into this world. We were not supposed to lose her.

We got back home around 5:30 in the morning still in such shock. Everyone was exhausted but sleep probably wasn't going to happen. I guess from pure exhaustion, I finally dozed off. After a couple hours, I woke up with pure panic running through my body. I jumped up and started calling Megan's phone over and over only for it to go to voicemail. I left messages for her asking her to call me because I had a horrible nightmare that something bad had happened to her. I knew she had plans to spend the night at the campground so I started getting dressed to go there and check on her. Dave came up and asked what I was doing. I said I had a horrible nightmare about Megan and told him that she wasn't answering her phone so I was going to the campground to check on her. He tried telling me it was not a nightmare, that it really happened.

I don't remember how, but the next thing I knew I was at the therapist's office. She started saying how sorry she was. I was trying to figure out what she was sorry for? I don't remember anything that she said or what happened there, but the next thing I knew we were back at home and people were calling and stopping over. There were hugs and tears and I started thinking that this could not be real. My insides were yelling, "NO! NO! I need to wake up from this nightmare! It's a beautiful summer day. What is going on?" My head could not wrap around the truth. Dave's brother and sister-in-law showed up with a plant, food, and more hugs and tears. Megan was really gone? Again, inside I was screaming, "NO!!" Later on, we had to decide what funeral home to contact for when they would release the body after an autopsy. We called the one right up the street from us and scheduled to meet with them the next day all the time in such disbelief that this is what we were doing on a beautiful Saturday.

Chapter 6

The Call: A Father's Perspective in Dave's Own Words

The interesting thing about life is everyone perceives it differently. When you're gathered around with your family reminiscing on past events there's always a 'that's not how I remember it' which graces the conversation. There will be different moment which stick with different people. Up to this point, you've been able to hear my wife's side of the story. All the events leading up to our happy life together. All the obstacles and memories up to the crash. I'd like to take a moment to tell you my account of the event.

June 24, 2016 started out like any other Friday as all woke up to begin their business for the day. Little did we know that by the end of that Friday every parent's nightmare would occur and everything would change. All who loved Megan would be devastated.

I was traveling to Northwestern Wisconsin to visit with my Mom who was in a nursing home. The plan was to have lunch and supper Friday afternoon, then stay at my sister's house. On Saturday, I planned to stop by to see mom again and then head back home in the afternoon.

My Mom and I had a great visit and around 8:45 pm. I said goodnight and headed to the local Walmart to get some items before heading to my sister's house. I had just checked out and was walking to the car when my phone started ringing. That was "The Call" that changed everything forever.

"The Call" was from my sister-in-law, and she indicated that there was a boat crash and that Megan was being administered CPR. I tried to get additional information, but at that time that was all she knew. She said she would call back as soon as she heard anything else and provide an update. At that point, everything seemed to be a blur, but all feelings and emotions went into hyperdrive. I had just been informed that Megan was involved in a serious crash and I was roughly five hours from home. Little was known about Megan's injuries and what was going on to take care of her or even which hospital the ambulance was going to.

At that time, my mind tried to convince me that this was just a dream and the crash did not happen. Once reality started to set in, my emotions took over and I began yelling, "NO! NO! NO!" over and over at the top of my lungs while sitting in the car in the Wal-Mart parking lot. The tears started and I began hoping against all hope that Megan was okay, and that I would be able to talk to her when I got back home and go see her in the hospital. I immediately called my Mom and let her know I needed to go home that evening and that I would not be seeing her the next morning. I did not let her know that Megan had been in a serious crash because I knew that would worry her so.

Prior to heading home, I again tried to find out which of the hospitals Megan was being transported to so I could go directly there to see her. Not knowing what hospital was very upsetting and added to the shock and pain regarding the news of the crash. As I headed out of the Wal-Mart parking lot, it still seemed like a terrible dream and that, really, everything was fine. I was quickly snapped back into reality and the grueling and emotional five-hour drive home to see Megan had just began.

The initial portion of the trip home was filled with desperately trying to comprehend the heartbreaking news. As it sunk in, I began to scream, "NO! NO! NO!" over and over in a painful way and could not stop sobbing and crying. I was desperately trying to find out what was going on. About one fourth of the way home, Robin got on the phone and said that Megan was gone. I couldn't and didn't want to believe it! The grief stricken NO! NO! NO! screams transformed into a low moan reflecting the grief and sorrow that began to consume my emotional and mental feelings. The trip home became a blur.

I began to remember our beautiful and precious Megan and the things that made her so special to me and all those who loved her. The realization that I would never ever receive Megan's random calls where she would say, "Love You, Daddy" or the random video calls with her three beautiful kids to chat was overwhelming.

In the midst of my anguish, the rest of the trip seemed so normal: road construction and stopping for gas while on the way, but nothing would ever be normal again. While stopped, I was able to get some more information, the hospital was insisting that Megan be transported to the morgue. The family requested that Megan remain in the hospital until I got home, but they continued to insist that she be transferred immediately. This meant that when I arrived home, I would have to go to the morgue to see Megan. I would have to go to the morgue to say goodbye to my daughter.

The five-hour trip seemed like it was an eternity and would never end. When I arrived home, the first thing I noticed was the large number of vehicles parked at the house. I had to park on the street in front of our house. I wiped the tears from my face and took a deep breath to try and compose myself and muster up enough strength to walk in the front door. As I entered the house, there was an eerie silence from all those that had come from the hospital and gathered to provide support and strength. Most were in the family room, and as I entered it seemed like all turned at the same time to look at me. I could feel the sadness and sorrow from all in the house regarding the loss of Megan.

When Robin and I saw each other, we stepped outside, hugged, and cried together for a long, long time. We then talked about going to see Megan at the morgue. We talked about how we would get there and how we would get into the building so I could see her. Our daughter Kristy offered to drive us to the morgue.

The morgue was a challenge to get directions to and locate. We also needed to identify whom we needed to contact to gain access to the building. As soon as we had that information, we headed to see Megan. The ride felt like an eternity and nobody said a word during most of the trip. Once downtown, we had difficulty locating the entrance door that was typically locked late in the evening.

We finally located someone that would provide access and we entered the building. This was one of the most difficult things I have ever had to do. I had to prepare myself emotionally and psychologically to see our Megan laying on the morgue table. When we were able to see Megan, it was worse than I ever imagined. A feeling of disbelief, sorrow, grief, and anger all rolled into one second. I never got to say goodbye or tell her one more time that I loved her with all my heart.

All I could do was stand there with our Megan and my insides exploded. You are not supposed to bury your child. Only those that have done so know and understand how this destroys your entire world and life as you know it from that point on!

Chapter 7

After Graduation

Yes, my husband is so right! A parent should never have to bury their child and only those who have done so can truly understand the grief that accompanies it. It's not the same as having to bury anyone else in your life, no matter how much they are loved. A child is someone who comes from you, they are a part of you and when you have to bury them it feels as if you're burying a part of yourself that will never be unearthed.

Before we go any further, I need to backup a moment so that you'll understand all that Megan left behind. It wasn't just me and my husband. Not just her two sisters. Megan had a family of her own as well.

After she graduated from high school, she decided to attend CNA School. She signed up for a six-week class, sailed through, got her license, and started working at a nursing home which she enjoyed. Unfortunately, she hurt her back and never went back. After she was feeling better, she took a parttime job where my son in law was working. It was a trucking place and she would make deliveries to customers.

While she was working there, she met a man named Erik who worked there also and before long they started seeing each other. Erik was a little older than Megan and had experienced his own tragedy. His wife had been killed in a car accident and left behind three little boys who now were without a mom. Erik had a lot he was dealing with but Megan and Erik seemed to like each other's company and before we knew it, Megan was pregnant. It was an unexpected blessing and on Oct 24, 2006, Ethan Michael was born and loved beyond words.

Although Megan was still living with us, Erik was still very much involved, and they were happy with this little addition. Ethan was a blonde haired, blue eyed, happy little boy who was adored by everyone. He was the perfect combination of his mom and dad.

Erik lived on a farm where he had cows and the boys would show them at local fairs. Megan loved the farm life. She was even able to get a couple of horses, which she had always wanted. On August 1, 2008, another little boy was added to the picture. Kaeden John was born. Megan adored her boys. Erik was now a Dad of five boys, and he adored the boys as much as Megan did. We were beyond happy with these two precious grandsons. They were happy, good, adorable little boys, but life is full of trials and sometimes things just do not work out as planned. Erik and Megan broke up. Then she decided to go back to school to get her associates degree. Erik was still very involved in the boy's life. They were such happy, fun little guys and it was working out well with them at home while Megan was working on her degree.

One night the boys were in bed and she asked if she could go meet some friends. I was in for the night so I said sure. I wanted her to go have fun. After she had been gone for a little while, she texted and said, "Guess who just walked in and bought me a drink?" I asked who and she said it was a guy named Robb from school who was her first serious crush. In no time, they were seeing each other pretty seriously, and she was happy to have reconnected with him. She had gotten her associates degree and had a good job by now. They got an apartment together and she was pregnant again. Their little girl was born February 15, 2012. They found a house they liked and moved in. He proposed to her and they got married in a beautiful outdoor ceremony on May 24, 2014. The boys adored their little sister. This next chapter of her life seemed to be full of beautiful promise. Then that awful night of June 24, 2016 happened

Chapter 8

Telling the Children

Megan's kids had to be told that their Mom was gone. How do you tell them something like that? They were 4, 7, and 9. The boys were on a camping trip out of town with their Dad and Megan's husband, Robb, had their little girl. Someone had called Erik and told him what had happened. I cannot even imagine getting that phone call where you are told that the mother of your boys is gone for the second time. I am not sure who made the decision but the decision was made to let the boys finish their camping trip. When they got back on Sunday, they would come to our house, Megan's daughter would be there, and they would be told all together. What a nightmare on top of the already existing nightmare that we were living. How do you explain this to them?

Erik and the boys arrived with two of their older brothers. Robb and their little girl were already there along with Megan's sisters. I remember some of the family stayed downstairs to be available after we told the kids so they would not be too overwhelmed by a crowd while receiving the news. We were sitting at the kitchen table. Robb was holding their daughter when Erik and the boys came in. I remember one of Erik's older boys sat down with Ethan on his lap. The brothers were older now and had been through this when they lost their Mom so they were there for their little brothers. Kaeden sat down. It was awful! We were about to crush these kids' lives. Nothing was ever going to be the same for them again. Their trusting little faces were looking at us, and we had to deliver the worst news ever. I still just wanted to wake up from this nightmare. How did this happen? I was feeling so sick. No one knew how to begin. I am not even sure who did begin. I just remember our granddaughter started crying, Kaeden was crying, and asking if the man who killed his Mom was in jail, and Ethan was on his older brother's lap trying not to cry but his face showed so much pain. Finally, the tears started. We were all trying to comfort them when we ourselves were in such pain. The rest of the family came up to the kitchen to try and comfort these precious kids whose lives were just changed forever. The nightmare continued. Everyone stayed for a while, then they left with the kids and we had to start planning a service. It was just one horrible thing after another.

Chapter 9

The Funeral

On Monday, an autopsy was performed on Megan. It was ruled that she had died from blunt chest trauma and on her death certificate, the cause of death was listed as homicide. There was such disbelief and a whole lot of anger. Megan was taken to the funeral home, and we began the process of planning our last goodbyes. I was in such a state of disbelief. I could not have done this without the help of family, especially my other two girls. Melissa, as hurt as she was, just took charge. Kristy, also in horrible pain, was here helping with this completely horrible time. Pictures were gone through, songs were picked out, an outfit for Megan to wear was chosen, and the pastor was called. All these horrible things that no parent should ever have to do were done while still in such disbelief and such horrible pain.

The visitation was going to be on a Wednesday from 4-8. The funeral home recommended this because they said since she was younger there would probably be many people so the visitation should be longer. The funeral home we chose was right up the street from our subdivision. We thought it would be good for us to be close to home. The day of the visitation, we were to arrive earlier for our private viewing of our daughter. There were so many floral arrangements that the funeral home said they were running out of space for them. So much love for our girl. Nothing, not even the visitation at a morgue, prepares you for seeing your child laying there in a casket; it takes your breath away. It is a horrible thing.

There sitting in her casket was "pink bear" a tragic reminder of how quickly life could come and go. I never would have guessed way back when she was five years old and wanted this $5.00 pink bear that it would become such a big part of her life. We all knew pink bear was exactly where Megan would want her stuffed friend to be, right there alongside her. We even cremated pink bear with her. She may have been an adult at the time of her death but I could still remember every detail of that five-year-old little girl, every detail of every moment from her short-lived life. My sister still has "blue bear" sitting on a dresser in her spare bedroom.

Around 3:30, someone from the funeral home came to us and said people were lined up around the building waiting for the visitation to begin. They were wondering if we wanted to start letting them in. We took our places in this horrible line to meet everyone who came to pay their respects to Megan. People started coming in and they just kept coming and coming. There were hugs, tears, words of comfort, and disbelief that this is what we were doing on this nice summer day.

Over 500 people showed up that night. It was supposed to be over at 8, but went on until almost 9. There was so much love for Megan, it was overwhelming but the support was so appreciated. When it was just immediate family left, we had asked if we could play one of Megan's favorite songs "Drink a Beer" by Luke Bryant and give a toast to Megan. They said yes, of course, so we brought in a cooler, everyone grabbed a beer or pop, we played the song, and toasted to our Megan. It was roughly 9:30 when we left the funeral home. It had been a long night but I was sure the night was going to be even longer. I was sure sleep was going to be impossible with what tomorrow was bringing. I kept thinking, "I can't do this! Last night was bad enough, I cannot say goodbye to my girl. Please let me wake up from this nightmare. This is not part of the plan for my life. NO!!"

I remember being in my bedroom the next day trying to get ready for this horrible afternoon that was going to happen whether I wanted it to or not. The girls were at our house by now and I was still upstairs in my bedroom. I could not breathe. I could not think. All I wanted to do was crawl back into bed. I could not decide what to wear. What do you wear to your daughter's funeral? This was not supposed to be happening. I just needed to wake up from this awful nightmare. Kristy came up to the bedroom and said, "Mom we need to be going," as I sat there on the edge of the bed still in my pajamas.

I said, "I can't. I don't know what to wear." She helped me pick out an outfit and get myself together as I guess people were already arriving at the funeral home. There was an hour visitation before the service and there were so many people. Megan would not have believed all the people that were there. Family, friends, and co-workers offered so much love and support. There were more tears, hugs, and still so much disbelief. What are we doing here? The service was going to begin so we took our seats in the first row, as the horror started. I was told later that the service was standing room only, again close to 500 people there for Megan. The pastor started talking, and then people got up to talk. Melissa spoke about Megan and their relationship. I don't know how she did it. I was totally in awe of her for being able to get through it. She had to stop a few times and take a big breath but she got through it. Other people got up and talked about Megan. We played her favorite songs and cried...a lot of tears.

I do not remember a lot about the service. One of her friends was recording it for us and I am glad he did. I could not watch it until I think the first anniversary of her death but he did a beautiful job capturing the music, the pictures, and the whole service. I cried ugly tears, gasping for air during the whole thing, but I was so glad that I had it because I didn't remember much from the service. I couldn't remember what people had said about Megan and as I sat there and watched this tape, it was so obvious that Megan was so loved and cherished by everyone in that room whether they spoke or not. You could feel the love and hear the sobbing of the people that were there because of Megan, our beautiful girl.

After the service was over, people started filing by the casket saying their final goodbye to Megan then coming over to us. I just sat there numb to what was happening. As the last person left, we went up to the casket, I just stood there not wanting to leave knowing I would never see her again. I could not leave. I could not leave her there. I was in such shock that this is what I was doing. Finally, I was led out to the car and we were headed to the luncheon for her where all these people would be. I was so tired, so numb, and wondering just how much more I could handle. The room was full again of people at the luncheon. All the floral arrangements from the funeral home had been delivered and I knew we had to get through this. The love and support from everyone was so amazing. Megan had touched so many people and was so loved. It was obvious from the outpour of support the last few days. But now it was over and we had to figure out how to live without Megan and how to start fighting for justice.

Chapter 10

The Fight for Justice Begins

After the service was over and we said goodbye to our beautiful daughter, we started hearing more about the man responsible for taking Megan's life, Marc Mongan. He was from a prominent family in the small town where the crash happened. We heard from friends that he was from money, owned his own pharmaceutical business and would probably just get a slap on the wrist. A life had been taken in this event, our daughter's, surely that wouldn't be the case. Everything inside of us wanted to believe that the justice system would do just as their name implied, provide justice.

At the hospital the night Megan was taken, the employee from the coroner's office had told me that the man responsible for the crash was in jail. We later found out that he was taken to jail and charged with operating a watercraft under the influence and reckless operation of a watercraft, both misdemeanors. We learned he was questioned by the arresting officer who had given him a field sobriety test at the crash site which he failed every part of. Eventually, he posted the $200 bond and went home. He never spent more than an hour in jail! He was probably back home before we had finished our visit at the morgue.

How does that happen? We had so many questions and were filled with even more anger! We knew he didn't get up that morning thinking he was going to kill someone, but his actions and choices on June 24, 2016 resulted in our daughter's death. To find out he had been home with his family while we were left saying goodbyes to our daughter in the morgue was maddening! Why did he get to carry on with life as usual while we planned a funeral still trying to wrap our heads around the total devastation none of us had planned to endure? Where was the justice in this? The mother inside of me wanted to scream. How could he even learn his lesson when there were no consequences for his actions? What actions were being taken to prevent him from carelessly bringing this devastation upon another family? He needed to be held accountable.

A few weeks after her death, we began asking more questions since we still hadn't heard from anyone yet. We called the state attorney of that county, SA Eric Morrow, and requested a meeting. In the meantime, we found out that under the current Illinois Boating Law (boating law 625 ILCS 45-5-16-a-B), if you are deemed under the influence of alcohol and there's a fatality due to the crash you give "implied consent" to a chemical test (alcohol or drug testing). However, upon investigation, we discovered this law was not followed with Marc Mongan the night he crashed into Megan. Although, the DNR Officer and Ogle County Sheriff contacted the SA Morrow and requested a warrant to complete the chemical testing on Marc Mongan they were denied by SA Morrow that evening.

Maybe, like us, you find yourself wondering why a warrant would be necessary if the law already states implied consent is given when a fatality occurs. From what I understood, this warrant ensures the accused party CANNOT refuse chemical testing. It is a bunch of legal stuff I do not understand to ensure that all the t's are crossed and the I's are dotted if the case goes to court. Yet here we were finding out that no chemical test, neither under warrant or implied consent, was done on Marc Mongan that night. Why? Our daughter was gone, a fatality had most certainly occurred, why wasn't this done?

When we finally met with SA Eric Morrow, we were provided with little clarity. As a matter of fact, all that meeting did was add fuel to the fire. We started the meeting by telling him we wanted justice for our daughter and were not going away. We informed him that even though we did not know him, we had been told Marc Mongan was a very influential person in the town where the crash occurred. For that reason, there were suspicions which lead us to believe the whole matter would be swept under the rug without any justice provided for Megan.

We asked if he was familiar with Mr. Mongan and he responded by letting us know he might recognize him if they passed on the street but they did not run in the same circles together. We asked if he was aware there was a street in the town named after Mongan's family. He responded that he didn't know about that. When we asked about the chemical test, he indicated he didn't have any information on that either. The entire meeting was so vague it only fueled our anger over the matter. How could he, a state attorney, have no idea who this influential man was? How could he claim to have no knowledge of a warrant he refused to issue? I left the meeting with a knot in my stomach. SA Eric Morrow had done little to assure me Megan would be receiving justice. I did not have a good feeling about him at all.

I later found out my mother's intuition had been correct. Eric Morrow and Marc Mongan had ties in numerous organizations, yet Morrow had said during our meeting they didn't run in the same circles and he "might" recognize Marc. Morrow said he didn't know about any street named after the Mongan family when in fact Eric Morrow lived on Mongan

Street right near Mongan's mother. Once we found this out, all my instincts were in full force. If this man would lie to us about something like not knowing about the Mongan street when he lived on it, what else would he lie to us about? As a state attorney, he was supposed to be Megan's voice; fighting for justice yet here he was lying to us about stupid things like a street name? How were we supposed to trust him? There was no chance we'd be trusting this man to fight for the justice Megan deserved. It was time we would take matters into our own hands. If the justice department wasn't going to do their job, we'd do it for them. We'd gather the facts and present them to anyone we could until Megan's case was heard and justice was served.

During our own investigation, we uncovered that the officer at the crash gave Mongan the field sobriety test, which he failed. After this, the officer made a call to SA Morrow informing him that he was sure the young woman involved in the crash was dead and Mongan had already twice refused a request for a breathalyzer. The next step was a chemical test which required a warrant. It was up to SA Morrow to call a judge and get a warrant but he failed to do so. This event was the beginning of injustice for Megan. The fight of our lives had only just begun.

Chapter 11

The Truth is

Revealed

We are just a Mom and Dad that have been forced into the "Bury Your Child" club that NO ONE wants to voluntarily join or be a part of. We have been forced to live through some of the darkest days emotionally, mentally, and physically that any parent may ever have to experience. The killing of our precious Megan was terrible enough but to then have the justice system devalue and disrespect her life during the criminal trial is unfathomable and difficult to comprehend.

We had and continue to have tremendous support and assistance from family, friends, county residents, and by all that loved and miss Megan each and every day. Our ongoing motto is "Minute by Minute & Day by Day" and the support is certainly what has assisted us in this world-shattering journey of grief and sorrow. Megan's death leaves a deep void in all of our hearts that we will struggle to fill for the rest of our lives.

We are now Megan's "Voice" and need to tell the story of this unbelievable journey and the many questions that need to be answered regarding decisions made by certain individuals within the Ogle County Criminal Justice System regarding this historic criminal case. We were able to personally observe the judicial process. We were involved in four individual meetings with State's Attorney Morrow (SA), Assistant State's Attorney Schuman (ASA), and Victim Advocate Candice Jackson as well 20 individual court dates.

There is no greater crime than to take another person's life. The other unthinkable crime is to then have the justice system sacrifice Megan by sentencing her killer, who plead "guilty" to a felony charge, to a sentence of 30 months probation. This confirms the prosecuting SA, ASA, and justice system's lack of morals after taking the ultimate oath to serve and protect the citizens within the county.

As Megan's voice, we want to start from the beginning with the initial face-to-face meetings with SA Morrow, ASA Schuman, and Victim's Advocate Jackson. We now see the many red flags as we reflect on those initial meetings that led to significant questions. In hindsight, it is clear that the outcome of this case was already predetermined the evening of June 24, 2016 when the boating crash occurred.

On that day, we experienced every parent's worst nightmare and our lives were turned upside down. Life as we knew it was destroyed forever. We immediately received calls from the local newspaper and news station media outlets regarding the boating crash that took Megan's life. We provided information about Megan and then waited for any information regarding the initial criminal charges in this brutal and senseless crash.

Prior to the initial meeting, we did a google search to learn more about SA Morrow and at that time, his 2016 Election Campaign Material included the following statement: *I WILL AGGRESSIVLEY PROSECUTE THOSE THAT DO YOU HARM.* When we saw this, our level of faith and trust in Morrow and the justice system was high. Little did we know how the case would progress and the decisions and actions that would be made that would contradict Morrow's campaign "slogan". Ultimately, the issuing of responsibility and accountability to the individual that took Megan from all of us would be handled in an unimaginable way.

Following are just a few of the important statements to keep in mind as additional information is provided regarding the decisions and actions by certain elected officials who had taken the oath to "Serve and Protect" the citizens who live in and visit Ogle County.

*The most recent 2020 Re-Election Campaign statements for SA Morrow included:

- *Genuinely Committed to Ogle County - Has Integrity + Dedication + Honesty.*
- *Eric (Morrow) doesn't need to make promises, his track record says it all.*

*The 8/24/2016 Winnebago Coroner's Inquest categorized Megan's death as a reckless "HOMICIDE" and Megan's Death Certificate indicates "HOMICIDE".

*During the 12/19/2016 meeting with SA Morrow, ASA Schuman, and Victim Advocate Jackson, Morrow verbally said to us, "THERE WAS NO CRIME COMMITED HERE".

*On 12/18/2020 Morrow was conducting a radio segment and I personally called in and posed the following question:

<u>My Question</u> – "In your Re-Election Campaign, how important is it to run the office in an ethical manner with integrity and trust that the voters expect out of the office?"

<u>Morrow Response</u> – "It is of utmost importance and <u>that is what we do every day.</u>"

*Because this crash occurred on the river, the overseeing agency with jurisdiction was the Illinois Department of Natural Resources (IDNR). As a result of the IDNR initial investigation, the following tickets were issued to the operator of the jon boat Marc Mongan who crashed into the pontoon boat Megan was riding on:

1. 2016CV52 WATERCRAFT OUI/ALCOHOL – Class A Misdemeanor (Ticket #569836)
2. 2016CV53 RECKLESS OPERATION/WATERCRAFT – Class A Misdemeanor (Ticket #: 569837)

*Illinois Boating Law indicates that FELONY charges should be issued if the following criteria is met due to the circumstances of the crash:

➢ Impaired (Issued OUI)
➢ Serious Injury and/or Death (Megan died as a result of the crash)

These circumstances warrant FELONY charges and the IDNR suggested the FELONY charges be issued but Morrow indicated to us that he did not want to "overcharge" in this case. These misdemeanor charges remained until Morrow recused himself from the case due to conflict of interest and/or suspected impropriety. The assigned Illinois Appellate Prosecutor immediately reclassified the original two misdemeanor charges to seven Felony Charges based on the documented evidence involving this case.

A key piece of evidence is the blood alcohol level of Mongan. Mongan denied two requests to take a breathalyzer and failed the field sobriety testing. With those facts, two very experienced officers from the Illinois Conservation Police and Ogle County Sherriff Office contacted SA Morrow by phone from the Ogle County Sherriff's office the evening of 6/24/2016 to obtain a warrant for the chemical testing of Mongan. SA Morrow refused to obtain a warrant and the result is that there is no documentation of Mongan's blood alcohol level. SA Morrow later documented that because there was no chemical testing (which was because he denied the warrant), the case that the operator was under the influence at the time of the crash would be challenging to prove.

The Ogle County Justice System prides itself on its commitment to serving the public by providing a fair and efficient system of justice that fosters the public trust and confidence. In our opinion, due to the documented evidence and questionable circumstances regarding this case, it would be prudent for the Ogle County Justice System to request an impartial and thorough investigation to prove that the judicial process was fairly and properly executed throughout the course of this case. This would solidify the legacy of the Ogle County Judicial Process.

We know we will never get our Megan back, but we will continue to dedicate our time and efforts to research and document the truth surrounding this case. The truth is in the evidence and this truth must be revealed so that Megan can truly rest in peace.

The next chapter is just the "Tip of the Iceberg" regarding this historic criminal case. The next chapters will expand upon some items mentioned and bring to light other key questions regarding the criminal case. It is our hope that What Was Done In the Dark – Will to be Brought Into the Light!!

Chapter 12

Court

This chapter focuses on the 20 court dates and significant developments that occurred during the criminal case and the "RED FLAGS" that surfaced during the case. The following represents a few of those "RED FLAGS" that cause us to continue to have questions regarding the decisions and actions taken in this criminal case by SA Morrow, ASA Schumann, individual Ogle County Judges, and the Judicial Process itself.

As we proceed through these red flag moments, it is important to note that in the initial stages of this judicial process, we were informed that the crash occurred in Ogle County. People familiar with Ogle County told us the crash would be "swept under the rug" with limited accountability, responsibility, and consequences applied because Marc Mongan was a prominent person and one of the "chosen ones" in Oregon, IL. In spite of being told these things, we continued to have faith and trust in the Ogle County Judicial Process, but little did we know that what people had told us was in fact true and Megan's killer would have limited consequences regarding the taking of Megan's life.

On August 9, 2016, I sent an e-mail to Victim Advocate Jackson, copying SA Morrow asking if the Ogle County State's Attorney's office had prosecuted a criminal case like this in the past? This question was to determine if the case should be moved to another jurisdiction. There was NO answer to this question. It was later determined that SA Morrow HAD NOT personally prosecuted ANY cases during his 6-year tenure as SA within the Ogle County State's Attorney's office.

On August 24, 2016, we attended the coroner's inquest meeting which presented its findings after reviewing the facts and evidence regarding the boating crash. The inquest results categorized Megan's manner of death as reckless **HOMICIDE** and this is listed on Megan's death certificate. The death certificate reflects the cause of death as being blunt trauma of the chest due to the boat striking her body during the boating crash. The results of the coroner's inquest was immediately e-mailed to SA Morrow on August 24th so he would be aware of this important finding and support a consideration to upgrade misdemeanor charges to felony charges.

RED FLAGS

SA Morrow, Ogle County States Attorney - Initial July 14th Meeting

When we heard the initial charges were misdemeanors, we could not understand why they were not felony charges since the crash resulted in the death of Megan and her death certificate indicated HOMICIDE as cause of death. We waited and waited to hear from the Ogle County State's Attorney's Office regarding the criminal case but did not receive any communication from SA Morrow or his office. We then had to look up information and contact SA Morrow's office ourselves to schedule a meeting to discuss the case.

On July 14th, 20 days after the crash, we finally were able to schedule a meeting at the Ogle County State's Attorney's office to discuss the criminal case and future actions that were to be administered to hold Megan's killer responsible and accountable for this tragic event.

Initial charges for Mongan included an Alcohol/OUI Misdemeanor Ticket which confirmed that he was deemed under the influence of alcohol while operating his boat that crashed into the pontoon boat Megan was riding on. During the initial meeting, we questioned what the BAL (Blood Alcohol Level) tests revealed as to the level of intoxication of Mongan. SA Morrow's response was that he was not aware if a breathalyzer or blood test was conducted to determine level of intoxication.

As the criminal case progressed, it was documented that SA Morrow had received a call from Steve Beltran, Department of Natural Resources Police, and Brian VanVickle, Ogle County Sherriff, requesting that a warrant be obtained to complete chemical testing of Mongan to document the BAC. SA Morrow *refused* to obtain a warrant to complete OUI testing which indicates he **was** aware that there was no OUI testing completed when he answered our question on July 14th. With no number available to document this BAC level, the table was set for how this case would proceed in the future.

The inability of Megan's killer to pass Field Sobriety Evaluations and documented statements by multiple police officers as to his level of intoxication prompted the OUI charge. During the initial investigation, it was documented that Mongan indicated that he had 6 drinks in the 2 hours prior to the crash.

The 6/24/16 Ogle County Sherriff's Office Narrative Report by Officer Deputy Thiel outlines some critical information regarding the crash as well. Deputy Thiel was the initial officer who was immediately with Mongan and documented crash information and observations regarding suspected influence of alcohol. Regarding intoxication observations the report states: "In talking with Mongan, I observed him to have glossy and bloodshot eyes. Mongan's speech was slurred as he talked, as if he was speaking with thick tongue. I noted a strong odor of an alcoholic beverage emitting from his facial area."

Mongan – Safe Boating Rule - Maintain Proper Lookout

The Code of Federal Regulations, Title 33 Navigation and Navigable Water – Coast Guard, Department of Homeland Security Regulation 33 CFR 83.05 – (Look-out Rule 5) states:

> "Every vessel shall at all times maintain a proper look-out by sight and hearing as well as by all available means appropriate in the prevailing circumstances and conditions so as to make a full appraisal of the situation and of the risk of collision."

Ogle County Officer Deputy Thiel's Report documents Mongan's comments that "He and his passenger were talking and not paying attention to the area. The boat operator stated that the next thing he knew they were striking another boat". It must be also noted that during the June 19, 2018 court date transcripts it is documented that Edward Fane (a good friend of Mongan) testified, "I know Marc telling me early on that he didn't see that boat".

This confirms that Mongan and Nick Lamb, other passenger in the boat, did not follow the safe boating rule of "Be Sure to Maintain Proper Lookout and Stay Alert" when boating on the waterways. The "Boater's Guide to the Federal Requirements for Recreational Boats and Safety Tips" indicates that "Most boating accidents are caused by operator inattention" which is documented in this case.

SA Morrow Supports Misdemeanor Charges (Does Not Want to Overcharge)

Although two misdemeanors were issued, IL Boat Registration and Safety Act. 625 ILS 45/5-16c was not followed because this law indicates that FELONY charges should be issued if the following criteria is met due to the crash:

- ✓ Operating a Watercraft Under the Influence of Alcohol (Issued OUI)
- ✓ Serious Injury and/or Death (Megan was killed because of the crash)

These circumstances warranted FELONY charges, and we were desperately trying to understand why the initial charges were not going to be upgraded to FELONY Charges. The IDNR Police suggested that FELONY charges be issued. The IDNR Police Officer called the State's Attorney's office and advised SA Morrow of the condition of Mongan and that he was involved in a boating crash resulting in a death. The IDNR Officer advised SA Morrow that Mongan was under arrest for Reckless Operation and Operating Under the Influence, refused breath, blood and urine sampling, and requested direction on additional charges. When we questioned why these were not upgraded to FELONY charges SA Morrow indicated to us that he did not want to "overcharge" in this case and with that decision, the charges remained Class A Misdemeanor charges.

SA Morrow Position "NO CRIME COMMITTED HERE!"

During a 12/19/2016 meeting with the SA Morrow, ASA Schuman and Victim Advocate Jackson to discuss the Grand Jury decision Morrow indicated to us that there was "NO CRIME COMMITTED HERE!" This position was completely unbelievable to us and at that point we wanted to get up to leave the conference room as we were totally devastated and upset regarding this statement. This demonstrated and validated the ongoing position of the Ogle County SA's Office regarding this criminal case.

At that time, I had a 5 X 7 picture of Megan in a frame and set it in front of Morrow on the conference room table and I said, "You tell her that there was NO Crime Committed Here". Morrow would not answer and in fact reached out on two occasions and physically pushed her picture away from him so he would not have to look at her photo. This comment and SA Morrow's actions opened our eyes wider as to the Ogle County Justice System and how they continued to disrespect and devalue Megan's life and all those who love and miss her each and every day.

SA Morrow - Refuses Request for Warrant to Conduct Chemical Testing

The significant question is why chemical testing <u>was not</u> completed on Mongan since he was deemed under the influence of alcohol at the time of the crash and this crash resulted in injury or death of a person.

The IL Boat Registration and Safety Act. 625 ILS 45/5-16c law indicates "By operating a vessel on Illinois waters, you have given "implied" consent to alcohol and/or drug testing if arrested for operating under the influence". IL Boating Law 625 ILCS 45/5-16-a- (B) confirms the "deemed to have given consent to a chemical test" regulation. Chemical testing is warranted if a boater is deemed under the influence of alcohol and there is **NO** option to refuse chemical testing. With this option, a warrant needs to be secured to complete the chemical testing. Morrow <u>REFUSED</u> the request to obtain a warrant. As already mentioned, with <u>NO</u> Blood Alcohol Concentration number to document Mongan's BAC level that evening a key piece of evidence was now missing.

IL Conservation Police Memorandum Dated 05/02/2017 (6 pages) documents "that there was no doubt a request for a warrant was made by CPO Beltran and was denied by SA Morrow. Sheriff VanVickle stated he would have no problem confirming those facts." It is important to note that this memorandum documents that SA Morrow indicated "I never denied a warrant for the blood" and SA Morrow "continued to call CPO Beltran a Liar".

Mongan Family Members at Crash Site

A person on the riverbank where the boats were brought in observed two females arrive very frantic and upset and one asked to see her Dad (Mongan). This witness heard the young lady indicate her Dad had called her and said another boat had hit him and for her to come to the crash site. The young woman was frantic and an officer she was standing by indicated she should go down and see for herself and then they could talk. She went down to the crash site to observe and speak to her Dad. She was not seen again so must have left the scene of the crash without talking to the officer.

It was later documented that Mongan had called his wife after the crash and that his oldest daughter had heard of the crash and both were present at the crash site. While at the crash site, Mongan had spoken directly to the oldest daughter. This would be critical evidence to assist in verifying the condition and level of alcohol impairment and/or intoxication of Mongan. This information was shared with SA Morrow and his response to my question about interviewing them was that "The Mongan family members would lie about what they saw or observed". Morrow decided not to follow-up or request an interview of these family members.

Mongan - Federal Law on Accident Reporting when Crash Involves a Death

Federal Law 33 CFR 173.53 requires the boat operator to submit a casualty or accident report to the State Reporting Authority (IDNR) when there is a death as a result of an occurrence that involves the vessel or its equipment. Immediate Notification of Death or Disappearance must be followed:

(a) When, as a result of an occurrence that involves a vessel or its equipment, a person dies or disappears from a vessel, the operator shall, without delay, by the quickest means available, notify the nearest reporting authority listed in appendix A.

A Freedom of Information Act (FOIA) request was submitted to the IDNR to determine if Mongan had notified and/or submitted a report this reporting agency. The response was that Mongan <u>had not</u> provided the appropriate notification of death to this agency. This is just another regulation that was not followed and for which Mongon was not held responsible.

SA Morrow - Denies the Review of Cell Phone Records (Call Log)

Mongan indicated that he was making phone calls with one being to his wife (Michelle) immediately after the crash. With this information, CPO Beltran seized Mongan's black Samsung brand cell phone for review in the pending investigation.

During the criminal case, we made numerous inquiries to SA Morrow and ASA Schuman regarding the phone calls and to whom additional calls may have been made that evening.

Both Morrow and Schuman indicated that Mongan's cell phone was "locked" and could not be opened to obtain call log data or any other information from the phone. They both indicated to us that to unlock the phone would be prohibited due to the needed technology and expense and that it would not be occurring in the future.

However, on 9/29/16 @ 2:27 PM a SEARCH WARRANT was issued by Judge John B. Roe indicating that this phone be searched and the following instruments, documents, articles, or items which constitute evidence of the offense: <u>Operating under the influence of alcohol or drugs</u> in violation of Illinois Compiled Statutes: 625 UK/CS 45/5-16(A)(1) be seized there from:

> Any and all data stored and or deleted on said device to include, but not be limited to: incoming and outgoing calls, text messages, images, video and/or voice recordings, phone numbers and contacts, locations, social media and internet histories and any and all date or information pertaining to the operation of a watercraft and/or the consumption of alcohol or drugs. This search warrant shall include authority to analyze and search any cell phone including the description of any encrypted data for relevant evidence as outline in this search warrant.

The cell phone was provided to the Northern Illinois University Department of Police & Public Safety to complete the data extraction process. On October 26, 2016 the cell phone passcode was overpassed, and the process was completed successfully, and data extracted included:

- 9   Audio Files
- 3   Databases
- 29   Documents

- 7849   Images
- 5   Text files
- 1456   Unassigned files

The forensic analysis was completed on the extracted data to parse and SIMS, MMS, calls logs and/or the passcode. Also completed a files recovery, forensic password attack, and binary index search. The determination revealed NO LOG for the SMS, MMS, calls log, and passcode. This produced another red flag. *There was no call log on the phone?* Was it erased? We repeatedly questioned SA Morrow and ASA Schuman regarding the call logs with each request declined by the Ogle County SA Office. During this criminal trial, these requests were declined, and they did not pursue this important source of evidence in the case. It was later discovered that Mongan in fact had two cell phones with him the evening of the crash and only one was turned in.

Mongan and Tess, Defense Counsel – Laughing and Joking in Court

During the October 11, 2016 Court Session we became terribly upset during the court proceedings. Judge Redington was proceeding through the initial cases when Mr. Tess, Mongan's lawyer, motioned for Mongan to come up to the bar that separated the lawyers and individuals in the gallery. When standing up in front of us they were smiling and laughing and then Mongan sat down. The death of our Megan is not a laughing matter to all that loved and cherished her. We had to leave the courtroom because we were so upset.

This behavior demonstrated by Marc Mongon and David Tess showed their lack of morals and how they devalued Megan's life. This outrageous display disrespected Megan and demonstrated that these court dates seemed to be just an "inconvenience" for Mongon.

SA Morrow & ASA Schuman – Grand Jury Process

SA Morrow and ASA Schuman had decided to convene a Grand Jury and present the extensive evidence and facts for a decision to possibly proceed in upgrading the initial Misdemeanor Charges to Felony Charges based on the decision of the Grand Jury.

As court designated "Crime Victims" we were supposed to be informed as to this decision and when the jury would meet to have evidence presented. The only notice we received was a November 30, 2016 e-mail from ASA Schuman stating, "I just wanted to update you on the Mongan investigation. Eric (SA) and I, along with Judge Hanson, selected and impaneled a new Grand Jury a couple of weeks ago for this investigation. We will keep you posted with any updates".

The next notification from SA Morrow was requesting a meeting on December 19, 2016. The Grand Jury had convened regarding the PEOPLE vs. Marc Mongan criminal case and he wanted to discuss the outcome. Heading into that meeting we felt confident that if the extensive evidence and in person testimonials by the three occupants of the pontoon boat plus other eyewitnesses there would be an important decision to further indict and Misdemeanor OUI + Reckless Operation of a Watercraft charges would be upgraded to Felony criminal charges. We traveled to Oregon, IL where the meeting occurred in the Ogle County Justice Center conference room. In the meeting were SA Morrow, ASA Schuman, and Victim Advocate Jackson.

During the meeting, SA Morrow discussed the presentation made to the Grand Jury to pursue Felony charges with additional elements which alleged that the defendant caused the death of Megan. SA Morrow's presentation of the evidence resulted in the Grand Jury finding *that there was NO probable cause to proceed with felony charges against the Defendant.*

With the extensive evidence and facts documented regarding this criminal case, we were undoubtedly surprised and disappointed regarding this decision. It was at this time SA Morrow said to our faces that "There was NO crime committed here". It was also at this time that I placed the framed 5" x 7" photo on the conference table in front of SA Morrow and said, "You

tell Megan!"

We were so devastated with this news and concerned about SA Morrow's behaviors that we both got up and left the conference room. On our travels home we heard on the radio that the news regarding the Grand Jury decision had already been provided to the news stations in the form of a prepared statement on the decision.

Our immediate question involved the Grand Jury process and what information was provided in order for the jury to make an informed decision regarding this criminal case. The most important question revolved around who was called to provide personal testimony to the Grand Jury regarding the facts and evidence involving the boating crash.

Our concerns increased once we determined that the occupants of the pontoon boat HAD NOT been contacted by SA Morrow or ASA Schuman to personally testify before the Grand Jury. We also found out that additional eyewitnesses and other individuals that were at the crash scene and could personally present additional information WERE NOT called by SA Morrow to provide important facts and evidence regarding the crash to the Grand Jury.

When we were informed of the decision by SA Morrow and ASA Schuman it was emphasized that the proceedings and documents surrounding the presentation of facts have been permanently sealed and could not be accessed for review in the future. This Grand Jury decision not to indict Mongan then became SA Morrow and ASA Schuman's "SHIELD" when answering any and all questions regarding this criminal case.

It was later discovered that the Grand Jury minutes document was filed on Nov 8, 2017 with the Clerk of the Circuit Court – Ogle County regarding Criminal Case-CF-168 which included a list of the following witnesses: Steve Beltran, Jennifer Kirchner, Matt Kirchner, Nick Lamb, and Dan Pierce. Jennifer and Matt Kirchner were friends of Mongan. Dan Pierce was in the area but was not an eyewitness to the crash. Nick Lamb was a friend of Mongan and the occupant in the boat when the crash occurred. Lamb indicated during the initial investigation interview with IDNR Officer Beltran "He stated they had been consuming alcohol and met with some friends on the river where they made additional drinks before traveling north toward the River Road Campground. Lamb identified the friends as Jennifer and Mathew Kirchner of Oregon".

This filed document verifies that though the occupant of the Mongon's boat was called to witness, the occupants of the pontoon boat that Mongan crashed into <u>were</u> <u>not</u> called to personally testify. It also verifies that others with important observations and evidence were not given the opportunity by SA Morrow and ASA Schuman to personally address the Grand Jury.

We wanted to know why SA Morrow and ASA Schuman did not include the pontoon boat occupants, additional eyewitnesses to the crash, Ogle County Sheriff's Police Officers at the scene of the crash, the Ogle County Sherriff who observed Mongan at the jail during the questioning by IDNR Officer Beltran, the IDNR Crash Reconstruction Specialist, or the coroner to review cause of death.

With the extensive amount of evidence why did the Grand Jury NOT return an indictment on the two misdemeanor counts? We have never had any negative feelings or ill will toward any of the Grand Jury members. The Grand Jury makes its decision based on the total evidence presented by SA Morrow and ASA Schuman regarding possible indictment. A major question is based on why there was NO indictment when Mongan eventually pled guilty to a FELONY charge which indicates the lack of presenting the appropriate evidence regarding this terrible crime to the Grand Jury. How could the grand jury make an informed decision if the presentation of evidence was compromised and not presented in its entirety? How can we trust that the Grand Jury process was conducted fairly and properly?

IMPORTANT NOTE

When SA Morrow and ASA Schuman recused themselves from this criminal case, it was assigned to David Neal, IL Special Prosecutor, who immediately upgraded the charges to 7 individual FELONY charges. Mongon ultimately accepted a FELONY Plea Bargain which confirms that he caused the death of Megan and emphasizes that this criminal case should have been immediately pursued as a FELONY criminal case based on the evidence. Even though he plead guilty, he was only sentenced to 30 months probation.

NICK LAMB – CRIMINAL vs. CIVIL TESTIMONY (DISCREPANCIES)

NICK LAMB - CRIMINAL CASE Testimony

During the Criminal Case, Lamb supported Mongan regarding his decisions and actions taken the evening of June 24, 2016 that resulted in the crash that took Megan's precious life. As documented in the June 19, 2018 court transcript the following statements were made:

David Tess, Defense for Mongan, indicated: "If you look a Nick Lamb's letter who was a passenger on the boat, his fishing partner, Marc (Mongan) <u>was in total control,</u> he was handling difficult maneuvers while they were putting out bait lines, changing complicated hooks on bait line. Nick Lamb's letter also indicated Mongon was "never irresponsible, never at a high rate of speed". These are just two of the documented comments by Nick Lamb supporting Marc Mongan regarding the evening of the crash.

NICK LAMB CIVIL CASE COMPLAINT AGAINST MARC MONGAN – CASE #2018L14

On 6/20/2018 (the day after Criminal Case Probation Sentence) Nick Lamb filed the following "COMPLAINT" with the Ogle County IL Clerk of the Circuit Court: Complaint: <u>Count I Negligence/Mongan.</u>

Included in the Negligence Complaints against Mongan are the following:

- ➤ That said Defendant (Mongan) operated and propelled that watercraft in such a negligent and careless manner so that as a direct result, Defendant's watercraft in which the Plaintiff, NICK LAMB, was a passenger struck another watercraft.
- ➤ That the Plaintiff, NICK LAMB, suffered physical, emotional, and permanent injuries.

> That the Defendant (Mongan) was guilty of one or more of the following, negligent and careless acts, or omissions to act:

   A. Operated the watercraft at a speed greater than would permit him in the exercise of reasonable care to bring the motorboat to a stop within the assured clear distance ahead in violation of 625 ILCS 45/5-1.

   B. Failed to signal while approaching an oncoming watercraft in violation of United States Coast Guard Navigation Rules.

   C. Failed to pass the oncoming boat without interfering with the path of that watercraft.

   D. Failed to signal his intent to pass the oncoming watercraft.

Shouldn't it be considered "Obstruction of Justice" since Nick Lamb documented two totally opposed testimonies during the Criminal vs. Civil Cases?

SA MORROW and DAVID TESS, DEFENSE, - CHANGE TO JUDGE REDINGTON

The PEOPLE vs. Marc Mongan criminal case has experienced a variety of Judges appointed to the case in the initial stages of this case:

Court Date	Judge
07/15/2016	Judge Kaufmann
08/08/2016	Judge Roe
10/11/2016	Judge Roe
12/12/2016	Judge Roe
02/14/2016	Judge Lindsey
04/25/2017	Judge Redington (Case progressed with Redington)

The 2/14/2017 Court Transcript documents SA Morrow and Defense Counsel Tess's statements regarding the transfer of the PEOPLE vs. Marc Mongan criminal case from current Judge Lindsey to Judge Redington.

Important excerpts from the Court Transcript includes:

➢ MR. MORROW: There has been a great deal of discovery. I'm not sure if all of it has been exchanged at this point, your Honor. I don't know if other reports are in or not. However, we have discussed continuing the matter on your motion to March 7th of this year at 2:00 p.m. in front of Judge Redington.

➢ THE COURT: Mr. Morrow, is that –

> ➤ MR. TESS: That's correct, Judge. It appears this case would be assigned to Judge Redington, we I think it makes sense to get in on his call. We have cleared with his clerk that date of March 7th at 2:00 p.m.

> ➤ THE COURT: The case is continued to March 7th at 2:00 o'clock.

Why would SA Morrow approve and jointly request this criminal case be transferred to Judge Redington's Court since:

1. Defense Counsel Tess and Judge Redington had been business partners in the Tess and Redington Legal Services business in Rochelle, IL and Oregon, IL area prior to Judge Redington securing the judge position in 2012.

2. Judge Redington has also been the presiding Judge on a previous case involving the pontoon boat operator.

3. Redington family members have been involved in past Morrow election campaigns.

4. Under Tess & Mass LLC it is documented that Defense Counsel Tess contributed to SA Morrow's Election Campaigns.

5. In a Ogle County Life SA Morrow 2020 Re-Election Campaign newspaper article it was noted in a photo that both Defense Counsel Tess & Crull are standing behind Morrow which indicates the ongoing support and relationship with SA Morrow.

If these do not indicated conflicts of interest, I don't know what does. Why would Judge Redington accept this criminal case with such a heightened appearance of impropriety based on past relationship with Defense Counsel Tess and SA Morrow? Conflict of Interest has many facets but the true test is that it leads to bias or making judgment and discretion decisions that favor one over another.

We believe that Morrow also had a conflict of interest. SA Morrow's decisions impacted the level of integrity, honesty, and credibility of the case. The following Morrow quotes outlined below support the decisions mentioned above and an apparent conflict of interest:

- "I know Marc. I know the Mongan family. Marc isn't going anywhere!"
- "There was no crime committed here!"
- "I did not want to overcharge!" "from OUI and Reckless operation of a Watercraft (misdemeanors to felony)

Morrow's decisions at the initial stages of this criminal case set the tone and wheels in motion to lead to a coordinated dismissal. This, to us, is Obstruction of Justice, Prosecutorial Misconduct and Ethics concerns that need to be investigated further. These are criminal charges that seem warranted in this situation.

SA MORROW – MOTION TO DISMISS INITIAL MISDEMEANOR CHARGES

On March 14, 2017, a <u>MOTION TO DISMISS AND OTHER RELIEF</u> was submitted by Tess & Crull LLC, on behalf of the Defendant (Marc W. Mongan) was filed on March 16, 2017 by the Clerk of the Circuit County Court of Ogle County. It is important to outline key paragraphs of the Defense motion to understand the response of SA Morrow:

MOTION TO DISMISS AND OTHER RELIEF

NOW COMES the defendant, MARC W. MONGAN by and through his attorneys, Tess and Crull, LLC and for this Motion to Dismiss, it states as follows

1. On or about June 27, 2016 the defendant MARC W. MONGAN, was charged with the following:
   a. Watercraft Operating Under the Influence (Class A)
   b. Reckless Operation of a Watercraft (Class)
2. That on or about December 2016, the Ogle County States Attorney's Office convened a Grand Jury relative to the incident which brought about the charges set forth hereinabove.

3. The charges presented to the Grand Jury were as follows:

   a. Felony Operating Watercraft Under the Influence (Class 2);

   b. Aggravated Reckless Operation of a Watercraft (Class 4).

4. The said Grand Jury did not return a true bill or indictment against the Defendant, MARC W. MONGAN

5. The only difference between the charges brought herein as a misdemeanor and those which could have been brought by any Grand Jury as a felony involving the same set of facts with the only additional requirement of proof being a death or great bodily harm.

6. That a death or great bodily harm is acknowledged by all parties

7. That the only probable cause issue the Grand Jury could have found would have been that of intoxication and/or recklessness

8. <u>That since there was no probable cause to return a true bill of indictment herein, there can be no probable cause for the misdemeanor offenses charged as set forth hereinabove.</u>

9. Paragraphs 9 – 14 are statements regarding suspension of driving privileges so proceeding to CONCLUSION statement of this motion.

WHEREFORE, the defendant MARC W. MONGAN, prays that this court dismissed all charges herein, rescind the statutory summary supervision and for such other relief as equity requires.

On March 30, 2017, a <u>PEOPLE'S ANSWER AND MOTION TO STRIKE PORTIONS OF DEFENDANT'S MOTION TO DISMISS AND OTHER RELIEF</u> was submitted by Eric Morrow, was filed on March 30, 2017 by the Clerk of the Circuit County Court of Ogle County.

It is important to outline key portions of the SA Morrow's Answer to understand the response of Morrow:

PEOPLE'S ANSWER AND MOTION TO STRIKE PORTIONS OF DEFENDANT'S MOTION TO DISMISS AND OTHER RELIEF

ANSWER

(Paragraphs 1 – 8)

NOW COME the people of the state of Illinois, by and through their attorney, Eric D Morrow, Ogle County States Attorney and for their ANSWER to Paragraph

1 – 8 of Defendant's Motion to Dismiss and Other Relief state as follows:

1. The people <u>admit</u> the allegations contained in Paragraph 1 – 8 of the Defendant's Motion to Dismiss and Other Relief.

MOTION TO STRIKE

(Paragraphs 9 – 14)

Paragraphs 9 – 14 are statements regarding suspension of driving privileges so proceeding to CONCLUSION statement of this motion.

WHEREFORE, the People of the State of Illinois request that the Court enter an order as follows:

A. Striking paragraphs 9 – 14 of the Defendant's Motion to Dismiss and Other Relief and granting no relief thereon.

B. <u>Granting</u> other further relief as the court deems equitable and just.

As we looked closely at this documentation, it seemed to be a roundabout way for SA Morrow to agree with the defense motion to dismiss all charges. We could see that they were continuing to use the Grand Jury decision as a vehicle to justify this course of action.

In SA Morrow's April 10, 2017 letter to us, he mentioned these two motions and the following paragraph summarizes his decisions regarding this criminal case:

> "The first argument is that the finding of the grand jury that there was no probable cause to proceed with the felony charges legally bars the state from proceeding with the misdemeanor version of the charges. Unfortunately, for the reasons addressed above, I believe that this argument may be well taken by the court and the charges could be dismissed. If the misdemeanor charges are dismissed by the court, we will be left with a situation where we are not legally able to proceed with either the felony or misdemeanor versions of the offenses".

It was these documents and this response which eliminated all trust and we then decided to contact other lawyers for possible representation as crime victims since SA Morrow and ASA Shuman were not representing Megan at that time. We were so upset with the Ogle County Judicial System process and determined we had to do something to be the voice for Megan as the criminal case proceeded. We are trying to understand the legal system and how it makes decisions that protect the residents of Oregon IL, Ogle County, and surrounding counties and "Prosecutes to the fullest extent of the law". We know we cannot turn back time to get our Megan back but we continue to have significant questions regarding how this criminal case was handled. This prompts serious questions about Ogle County Law Enforcement and the current judicial process regarding the equal and impartial rights within the Ogle County Justice System.

CHAPTER 13

Trying to Survive

June 24. The dreaded date of the horrible night that one person's poor decisions took our Megan and changed our lives and so many others forever. Five years this year, at times it's so hard to believe it's been that long since all new memories of Megan have stopped. No texts, no phone calls, no recent pictures of Megan, so many days that she wasn't there, so many moments of her kid's lives that she hasn't been there for. Then other days it still seems like it was yesterday, the pain is still so raw, that awful night still plays over and over in our minds. The numbness and denial are gone - we live everyday with the pain that Megan is gone. We'll never see her again in this lifetime. Her kids have to grow up without their Mom. We have to live every day with a huge hole in our lives and hearts. The pain doesn't get easier. The saying that "it gets easier with time" is just wrong. Time has not lessened the pain at all. Sometimes I think time makes it worse, I dread every June 24th for more than one reason. I hate saying Megan has been gone another year, another year of missed holidays, birthdays, her kid's lives, just every day stuff, no more pictures of Megan's smiling face, or family pictures, how does that get better? Time has just allowed us to try to figure out how to go on day after day missing all this, to exist without one of our girls, to always have this horrible pain right under the surface no matter what we're doing.

It has changed who we are, it has changed so many relationships in our lives, a few for the better, some are strained and probably always will be, some unrecognizable, some just nonexistent. We are not who we used to be. The anger towards the corrupt justice system in this case simmers inside us.

We were told a couple times by the Ogle County system that this was just a horrible accident. It was not an accident and we never use that word. It was a horrible crash that was 100% avoidable. It was no accident that the man responsible chose to drink that day. It was no accident he chose to get behind the wheel of a boat. It was no accident that witnesses have said that he chose to meet up with another boat and have drinks with them. It was no accident he didn't have a lookout on his boat. It was no accident he was driving his boat at such a high speed that his words were "he never saw a pontoon boat" in broad daylight and he hit it so hard that his boat didn't just hit the pontoon boat, it went up on the pontoon boat, striking Megan in her chest area with his boat and throwing her into the river before his boat came back down in the river. People were frantically looking for Megan in the river before they found her face down in the water and jumped in to get her and pull her onto another boat who had come out to help and start CPR on her. This crash was totally avoidable. It should have never happened. Megan had to have an autopsy and then a coroner's inquest which consisted of six people who went over everything. She died due to blunt chest trauma. She had always wanted to be an organ donor, she was adamant about this, but because she died instantly, and there was so much damage to her major organs, they were only able to use her coronas and bone marrow.

The coroner's inquest ruled her death HOMICIDE. Her death certificate says HOMICIDE on it. How is someone not responsible? Nowhere does it say anything about this being a horrible accident. The person responsible never spent an hour in jail because of who he is and who he knew. If he wasn't impaired and it was just a horrible accident why refuse a chemical draw? Why didn't SA Morrow do his job and get a warrant for a chemical draw? What were they so afraid of?

At one time, an officer told us that if it had been the other way around and the pontoon boat driver had killed someone on the other boat he would be in prison. So why not even an hour in jail for this guy? He posted $200 on a Friday night and was home with his family before we left the morgue that night with a part of our family gone forever, so yes there is a lot of anger. The system should be the same no matter who you are or who you know especially when it involves something as serious as causing a death.

The law needs to be followed exactly the way it is supposed to be with no exceptions especially when a life has been taken so senselessly. Megan's Dad made a promise to her at the morgue that night that he would get justice for her, and we have tried every day since that night for justice but it's really hard when you're up against a corrupt system that has a SA who wouldn't fight fair and who wouldn't do his job and get a warrant. The man who killed Megan would have totally had everything dropped in April of 2017 if we had not finally found an attorney who was as outraged as we were and joined us in the fight for justice for Megan.

We hired her the night before court and she became Megan's voice and fought like hell for Megan. The fight continued with this determined attorney on our side, but again we had no chemical draw to prove his intoxication that night even though at the scene there was a field sobriety test performed on him and he failed every part of it, it wasn't enough. For over two years we made countless trips to Ogle County, a 45 minute drive one way from our home, just to watch this man get special treatment, come in the back door of the courthouse so he wouldn't have to face the supporters of justice for Megan outside of the courthouse, and leave court occasionally through the judge's chambers. He never came out of the courtroom as we sat in the hallway devastated at what just took place. He was never in the courtroom until after the judge was present. He never showed remorse at all in front of Megan's family as we sat there trying to keep it together.

At one court date, his attorney and him were talking quietly and then started laughing in front of us. I was so upset that they could laugh in front of us as if nothing was really wrong, that I had to get up and leave the courtroom for a while. All the time we were pushing for a trial. We wanted a trial so evidence could be shown, testimonies could be heard, and things could be done the way the law intended. In the end, he took a plea deal for the lesser of the charges and got 30 months of probation from a judge who used to be law partners with this Marc's attorney. Thirty months of probation for taking our daughter and changing so many lives forever. That probation was up in December 2020.

The pain of losing a child is indescribable. It's like no other. We both had lost our dads before Megan and it hurts, but it is the natural part of life's circle. You know you will bury your parents someday, but it is unnatural to bury your child. We have known people who have lost a child. A couple of Megan's good friends in school died before they even graduated and my heart hurt for them. I went to their services, I cried, I lost sleep, but I had no idea what those parents were going through. It is a club that no one wants to be in and once you are in it, there is no escaping. I do not want anyone I know to ever experience this nightmare of child loss and I think that is why so many relationships, even the closest ones change. They cannot understand and you are thankful that they are not in this horrible club but there is no way anyone can know what you're going through every day. Even on a somewhat good day, the hurt of your child not being there is right under the surface, the pain ready to explode at any given moment. Even special occasions are hard because the thought that someone so important is not there is always present. Even the simplest task like shopping can turn into a panic attack because all of a sudden I'll see something that Megan loved and I would have picked it up for her once again realizing I'll never be able to give it to her. I have left many stores without purchasing what I had because the tears start, my heart races, and I know I have to get out and be alone because people won't understand what is happening. Everyone grieves differently, there is no right or wrong way and no one should be made to feel bad for the way they are grieving. We need comfort, a shoulder to cry on, and someone to listen to our outrage without judging. That outrage can come out when it shouldn't. At times I've yelled when I shouldn't have and been short for no reason except missing my daughter. I've shut down at times when it wasn't the best time. I've cried over the stupidest things. I've pushed people away because I hurt so bad and I know they can't get it. We can be having an OK day and some little thing will trigger us like a song Megan liked or finding something of hers. I could be anything really, and instantly that day changes into a really bad day. Dave's line is "minute to minute" not day-by-day. I have no energy and some days I still just want to curl up in my bed and cry for Megan.

Things that used to be important in life are not so important anymore. I could not care less about the dust but instead care more about things I never thought of before like keeping my daughter's memory alive, about the laws being the same for everyone, about her kids growing up without their Mom, and about who I used to be. I don't even know who that person is anymore. I don't remember what it felt like not to have this constant hole in my heart, the ache in my soul, and my brain replaying that night over and over. I know I'll never see that person again. She's gone. She left that night when I was told that Megan was gone, and I know her Dad has these same feelings. We just express our grief differently. Child loss is unbearable and it never leaves you for a second. It's always there. Be patient with us.

Megan was special as are my other girls. We were blessed with Megan for almost 32 years, which I hold every second of tightly, but she should still be here with us. Almost 32 years isn't enough! It's not natural for parents to bury their children. When she was taken so much of us went with her. Parents that experience child loss are different. It's a depression that can't be fixed with medicine. I know I have fought depression my whole life, been on all kinds of different medicines, but nothing compares to this kind of depression. Your physical body is just a shell for the broken heart and for the traumatized brain that won't stop replaying the loss of your child. The what if's? There are days you wish you could just sleep and shut out the outside world. There are days you don't want to shower, get dressed, or even eat. You turn the TV on just for the noise so maybe it will drown out the nightmare that keeps playing in your head. I have had lots of these days, and still experience all of this today and people don't get it, especially because it's been five years since Megan was taken. They don't understand how you haven't been able to move forward even a little. I still have so many days I can't think straight and can't remember the simplest of tasks that I've done forever. I feel like I am losing my mind and feel so fragile. I carry a fake smile and try to act like I'm okay but the truth is I am not okay and never will be again. My child is gone. How can I ever be okay? Everything just keeps going around in circles. Most days I try to function like everyone else but there are days that physically, my mind and body are telling me something else. It's too hard some days to carry that fake smile and put myself together even around loved ones. It's not on purpose. It's that part of me that has been ripped away and I will never be able to get it back.

People take offense when our grief takes over and we shut ourselves in. Even this last Mother's Day, which was my fifth Mother's Day without Megan, started out rough. As I was reading texts from my other girls and feeling the love from them a little piece of me kept waiting for the text from Megan. Then the tears started rolling down my face because I knew that text would not be coming and the sadness set in and I just wanted to scream. It's so unfair but you let those tears roll down your face then force yourself to get ready because you're going to see your other girls and grandkids and they make the day better. Then comes a sign from Megan to let you know she is there. I look for those signs from her and I know she sends them especially when I need them the most. All we ask is for patience and a little understanding and not to take it personally especially on these days when reality hits like a slap in the face. The reality that she's not going to be there to celebrate with you and never will be again, and as much as you look forward to seeing the other girls and grandkids, which are a true blessing, a piece of your soul will not be there and it hurts. It is such a physical hurt, such a disbelief still that she is gone. We need our space at times. We have lost personal relationships because they do not know how to accept the new broken people that we've become. Unfortunately, we will continue to be broken. The grief will never leave me and it's simply because I love my child more than I could have ever imagined and I say it in the present tense "love". It is excruciating knowing Megan is gone after almost 32 years, but our love for her will never be gone.

I know it is difficult for people to understand our ongoing grief. I guess because they want us to "get better" or return to who we used to be. Every day is tough but holidays, birthdays, and the day she was taken will never be the same for us. We do the best we can. We try to celebrate the holidays and the birthdays with our loved ones, but right under the surface is the horrible pain and the reality that Megan is not here with us. It just does not go away, no matter how many holidays and birthdays have gone by. It is always there right at the surface ready to explode because the pain is so unbearable.

Grief is kind of like the weather. Some days it is calm and quiet. Other days it is a devastating storm that makes me feel so angry, exhausted, raw, and empty. I never really know what kind of day it's going to be when I wake up. I wake up in the morning and wonder, "how am I supposed to make it through another day?" I get up and try my best to cope with whatever the day brings. Some days are a little easier than others, but really I am just hoping that the grief storms stay at bay. With our grief, there are so many confusing contrasts. They are like undercurrents that tug at our hearts and minds. We are parents of a child who is not here anymore. Perhaps a child who you have never met. You cannot know how special she was or how her smile lit up the room, or her witty sense of humor. You cannot know how she won't watch her kids grow up and she'll miss so many of her kids' milestones. People don't realize that I grieve for each of her children's milestones that they'll have without their mom there knowing they didn't get the opportunity to experience these special days with her.

After Megan was taken, the first time I was asked by someone "how many kids do you have", I felt like I had been punched in the stomach. I couldn't breathe. I mumbled something and darted knowing a panic attack was coming on taking over my body. I didn't know how to answer, what if they asked where they live, or how old are they? How do I explain? It didn't take long for me to know how to answer this question if it came up again. I will always answer that I have three amazing girls. Another thing that was said to me shortly after Megan was taken that took my breath away was "thank god you have two other girls". I know how lucky I am to have my other girls and

I honestly don't know how I would have survived without them. I love each one of my girls. They are all special in their own way but one of my girls is gone so please be careful with comments like these because it's difficult enough for us who often feel torn between feeling happiness and joy for our other two living girls and the grief we feel because Megan is gone. Sometimes I feel people are afraid or uncomfortable bringing Megan up. Please don't be. We love it when someone says Megan's name and talks about her. We love hearing stories about her no matter if we have heard them a hundred times or maybe you know a story we've never heard. We want to talk about Megan. Our biggest fear is that she will be forgotten (which we know she won't be) and when time goes by without hearing her name it saddens us. We want to talk about Megan, might be a few tears shed but knowing she's not forgotten means a lot to us.

Chapter 14

No Justice is Injustice

JUSTICE

"Lady Justice" is typically recognized as the moral compass and devotion to the objective truth across all judicial systems. She is the ultimate symbol of impartiality and fairness that applies to everyone regardless of power, religion, race, stature.

Lady Justice

fair and equal administration of the law without corruption, favor, greed, or prejudice

Lady Justice also symbolizes the highest level of morals to the fair and equal administration of the law, without corruption, favor, greed, or prejudice for those who practice law and enforce justice.

INJUSTICE

Injustice is defined as a specific unjust act; a wrong or a violation of right or of the rights of another. Injustice is also defined as, "not based on or behaving according to what is morally right and fair."

We were desperately hoping that Lady Justice would join us in our "Stand Up for Megan" journey. We quickly learned that those that made the willful and wanton decisions during this case violated many of the oaths that they took to serve and protect the victims of violent crimes. We began to realize that the serve and protect process was not for Megan but for Marc Mongan with repeated statements that Mongan has rights. What about Megan's right to live a long and productive life with her kids and family? That did not seem to matter as we continued to have questions why key evidence was not considered and/or "swept under the rug" so Megan's killer would not be truly held responsible or accountable for the homicide that took her life.

WHEN a HOMICIDE is NOT a HOMICIDE!

The definition of HOMICIDE is when one human being causes the death of another. Megan's death certificate categorized her death as a HOMICIDE and it is difficult to understand why this criminal case was not initially pursued as a HOMICIDE case. It is also difficult to understand that a felon can plead guilty to a plea bargain on "COUNT 6 - RECKLESS CONDUCT" charge regarding Megan's death and the consequence is a 30-Month Probation Sentence with "no time in jail".

FELONY COUNT 6 Charge Includes:

On or about June 24, 2016, in the State of Illinois and the County of Ogle, defendant MARC MONGAN, committed the offense of:

RECKLESS CONDUCT

(CLASS 4 FELONY)

in that he, while acting in a reckless manner, cause great bodily harm to Megan Wells in that he operated a watercraft, a 2002 during craft at approximately 3400 North River Rd. on Rock River, in the city of Oregon, Ogle County, Illinois, without giving the required right of way to another watercraft, at a speed which was greater than was reasonable and proper with regard to the existing boating conditions and the safety of persons or property upon the waterway, causing his watercraft to strike the person of Megan Wells, thereby causing the death of Megan Wells.

In violation of SECTION 12 – 5(A)(2) of ACT 5, CHAPTER 720 of the Illinois Compiled Statutes.

There is no greater crime than to take a precious life! The 30 month probation sentence does not seem to be an appropriate consequence for taking Megan's beautiful life. It is understood that part of Marc Mongan's probation includes community service which included painting fire hydrants in the city of Oregon, IL. Painting fire hydrants for taking a life! Does that seem OK with everyone?

These types of criminal cases should <u>never</u> be compromised by the judicial process. The Ogle County Justice System "Crossed the Line" in this case by demonstrating that it is acceptable to take a life and the consequences will be little or no responsibility or accountability for those criminal decisions and actions.

We certainly feel that the willful and wanton decisions and actions taken by those who have disrespected Megan, devalued Megan's life, and ultimately "Sacrificed Megan" for one of their chosen ones has compromised the Ogle County Judicial

System. Their professional and personal reputations and these decisions and actions will now be their future legacy.

This criminal case exposes a double standard of justice and has destroyed confidence and trust in the fair administration of justice. This double standard sends an unforgettable message regarding SA Morrow's, ASA Schuman's, and the Ogle County Justice System's integrity, dedication, honesty, values, and morals dedicated to human life for those who live in Ogle County and those who visit the area.

Justice or Injustice

This and previous chapters have outlined a significant number of documented situations in which some serious questions emerge regarding justice and injustice? Since so much information has been given, it is important to review each scenario and then categorize and compile perceptions on the process. A decision can then be made regarding the evidence and information to determine if the actions taken by those who took the oath to "Serve and Protect" followed the Lady Justice principles for an objective and fair process were followed.

To question the fair, ethical and unbiased process of justice we can initially consider this Hypothetical Question:

1. Hypothetical Question – If anybody else had been the operator of the flat bottom jon boat that crashed into the

pontoon boat taking someone's life would they receive the same judicial process and ultimate consequences?

If the answer is NO this strengthens the evidence that questionable decisions were made and judicial process was unjust in this criminal case.

Our Opinion – The boat operator causing the crash would have been immediately put in jail and charges would be Felony OUI + Reckless Homicide and the consequences would be a lengthy prison sentence had it not been Marc Mongan.

Under the Influence of Alcohol Evidence "Swept Under the Rug"

The Felony Plea Bargain #6 RECLESS CONDUCT "Did Not" include any reference to Marc Mongan operating the boat while under the influence of alcohol. This despite the overwhelming evidence since the consumption of alcohol was a significant factor in this boating crash.

In a April 10, 2017 letter from SA Morrow he documents the following statement: "The totality of the evidence indicates that the Defendant did consume alcohol on the night in question". Marc Mongan also indicated during the investigation that he had consumed 6 drinks in the 2 hours prior to the crash. The passenger in the boat with Marc Mongan also documented that they had been consuming alcoholic beverages prior to the crash. Marc Mongan refused 2 requests by police to take a brethalizer. Marc Mongan also failed every portion of the field sobriety evaluation conducted by Steve Beltran, IL Department of Natural Resources Police Officer. One of the initial Misdomeaner Charges was "Operating a Watercraft Under the Influence of Alcohol". Vehicle Etc. Etc.

The important question is "why" was the consumption of alcohol "Swept Under the Rug" during the evolution of this criminal case? It is interesting to note that David Tess, Defense Council, indicated during the Court Date Sentencing Hearing no less than 3 times to Judge Redington that there was "NO ALCOHOL INVOLVED" in this crime. After the sentencing hearing David Tess also mentioned to the media on camera the same "NO ALCOHOL INVOLVED" statement. These statements directly contradict the overwhelming evidence regarding the consumption of alcohol by Marc Mongan the evening of the crash.

We are still trying to understand why it is acceptable and condoned for the Defense Council to blatantly and emphatically "not tell the truth" regarding the documented evidence in this case?

SENTENCING – OK to Take a Precious Life Since it is an "Aberation" of Behavior

Prior to the sentencing Judge Redington indicated the following statements on key factors discussed during the session as documented in the June 19, 2018 Court Transcript:

"Our law <u>allows</u> for the concept that a person can commit an offense that is an aberration to his or her character over time and have that considered, I do consider that:"

- ✓ Factor A-8, States that the defendant's criminal conduct was a result of circumstances unlikely to reoccur. I do believe that that's been shown.
- ✓ Factor A-9, I do believe that the character and attitude of the defendant indicate that he is unlikely to commit another crime.
- ✓ Factor A-10, I find the defendant is particularly likely to comply with the terms of probation.
- ✓ Factor A-11, I find the imprisonment of the defendant would entail excessive hardship to dependents.

Having reviewed all the statutory factors that I'm required to consider, it is a sentence of this court that:

"Mr. Mongan, you will be placed on a period of Probation for 30 months until December 19 of 2020. Conviction will enter on this felony, and whatever consequences that come within that come with that. You will be subject to the general supervision of the probation department. You will not violate any criminal statute of any jurisdiction."

Aberration Definition- The fact or an instance of deviating or being aberrant especially from a moral standard or normal state of character. Something or someone regarded as atypical and therefore able to be ignored or discounted.

QUESTION - Does 30 Months Probation seem an acceptable sentence when a person takes a Felony Plea Bargain indicating that his reckless conduct caused the Homicide Death of Megan (Swaziek) Wells?

Behaviors That Are Rewarded Will Continue

Another major concern is that those with power and influence made decisions that "Cross the Line" when a crime involves a fatality. This demonstrates the willful and wanton actions exercised in cases of this type.

When this behavior is elevated to the unforgivable level it will typically be replicated on other criminal cases of a similar nature. With that in mind, it will be important to review and evaluate if similar decisions and actions were taken on past criminal cases. When an individual has immunity regarding their decisions of this type the hope is that they make the proper and ethical decisions while in the position of power and influence. These decisions and actions must also be ethical and trustworthy on each and every criminal case within their jurisdiction. The odds of similar unethical behavior is significantly increased especially if the individual is not held responsible or accountable for those that compromise a criminal case.

Special Non-Biased Investigation Required

The Ogle County Justice System indicates that it prides itself regarding its commitment to serving the public by providing a fair and efficient system of justice that fosters the public trust and confidence. Due to the documented evidence and questionable circumstances regarding this criminal case we are requesting a thorough, nonbiased, and impartial investigation to prove that the judicial process was fairly and properly executed throughout the course of this criminal case. This investigation should also be expanded to include past criminal cases of this type. This would answer the questions and solidify the legacy of the Ogle County Judicial Process.

The willful and wanton decisions and actions by those who are responsible to "Sacrifice" Megan demonstrate the depth and breadth of the injustice perpetuated that violated Megan's and our constitutional rights by the intentional and reckless infliction of emotional pain.

When SA Morrow and ASA Schuman said to our faces "THERE WAS NO CRIME COMMITTED HERE" this statement was certainly incorrect since Marc Mongan plead "Guilty" to a Felony Charge. This is Textbook Prosecutorial Malpractice and documents the "Injustice" surrounding this criminal case.

We continue to try and recover from this nightmare and this has rekindled the fire and desire to obtain "Justice for Megan" by bringing "What Was Done in the Dark - Into the Light" so she can truly rest in peace.

We will continue being the voice for Megan since she does not have one during this "Justice for Megan" journey.

For detailed information and documentation go to the www.StandupforMegan.com website.

Chapter 15

The Final Chapter

In closing, we want to say that the Ogle County Court System let this injustice happen, however during this horrible ordeal we have had so many Ogle County residents reach out to us and support us, letting us know that they believe there was no justice served and that Marc got off way too easy. We appreciate the amazing support from these people who we did not even know.

A special thanks to Joy and her husband Don. Joy was at every court date supporting us the whole time. We didn't even know her before this tragedy but she saw the injustice and took time out of her days to be there for us. She did whatever she could to help. Thank you! Without all the support that we have received during this ordeal from people who have reached out to us and to our family we would not have had the strength to continue. To the 500 plus people who have joined the Justice for Megan facebook page, we cannot say thank you enough. It means so much to us to see that we are not alone in the outrage that we feel. We are not just grieving parents, reaching out. This really is a horrible injustice that was done to Megan and our family and it could happen again if something does not change. The law should apply to everyone no matter who they are or who they know. There should be accountability and justice for a life taken. Megan didn't get that!

A very special thank you to our daughters Kristy and Melissa who are also struggling with a huge void in their lives after losing their sister. They stepped in from the moment it happened, being there for us, taking care of things, and taking care of us while dealing with their own horrifying grief. We love you both more than you'll ever know.

To our beautiful grandkids who make the world a better place. Kristy's three amazing kids, Dylan, Kaitlyn, and Kara and Megan's three awesome kids, Ethan, Kaeden, and Robbie Marie you are all such a blessing. Last but definitely not least last November our youngest daughter Melissa and her husband had their first baby. A beautiful little girl whose name is Olivia Megan after her Aunt Megan. Melissa and Megan were more than sisters, they were best friends and this sweet little girl has a very special guardian angel with her always. She will know her Aunt Megan through all of us and we know her Aunt Megan is watching over Olivia Megan. You are all loved more than you'll ever know. You make our hearts feel love and joy even on our darkest days.

To Dylan - my rock! There are not enough words to say how special you are. I don't know what I would have done that horrible night without you. That awful night is just a nightmare playing over and over in my head with some of it fuzzy because I couldn't believe what was happening. Some memories are so real, images of Megan laying there burned in my memory forever but the one constant thing I remember is you by my side the whole time, holding my hair while I had my head in a garbage can being sick, holding me when I felt like my legs were giving out, and answering my phone. Then going with us later, along with Kristy and Melissa, to the morgue and keeping it together for us. At the service you never left our sides at all while all the time your heart was also broken from losing "Aunt Mer " and when I think back and realize you were only 17 years old, the maturity you showed and the comfort you gave us is just indescribable. Thank you just doesn't seem enough. You are my rock and always will be. Aunt Mer would be so proud of you.

Also for all the other numerous family members who were at the hospital that night, the love for Megan and the support you all showed are beyond words. Megan was so loved.

Attorney Cindi Koroll there are no words to express what you mean to us. You took on this fight when no one else would even talk to us. You put your heart and soul in this case for our daughter. Your fight and determination for justice will always be the reason this case wasn't dismissed in just misdemeanor charges. You weren't just an attorney doing a job, you were fighting for Megan. We know this wasn't just another case for you. We are forever grateful for everything that you've done for us and for Megan. You were her voice, her angel. You are still a very special person in our lives. When the case was over you didn't just put it away and forget about it. You're always there for us and you come to Megan's birthday celebrations. Even though you never met Megan personally, I know you will never forget her. Thank you from the bottom of our hearts. You started out as an attorney for us, but now we consider you as so much more, we consider you as a dear friend.

Finally, people just can't believe some of the stuff when we tell them what went on in this case. If you still wonder about certain things or find this so unbelievable, please feel free to check out the website, www.standupformegan.com. Read the reports and watch the videos for yourself and then ask yourself, what would you do if this was your daughter? Join the facebook page "Justice for Megan". Any questions or comments you can contact me at robinswaz@hotmail.com or her Dad at dmswaz@comcast.net

Megan will not ever be forgotten, we will continue to keep her memory alive and fight for the laws to be the same for everyone, especially when a beautiful life is taken. We love you, Megan.

With the loss of Megan our hearts are and will always be broken beyond repair, leaving a huge hole that will hurt forever. Her family and friends will never be the same after losing Megan, losing her smile, her spirit, and her specialness. We cherish new memories made with our other girls and our grandchildren but always with the knowledge that there are no more new memories with Megan. There will be no more pictures of her, no more texts just to say hi or I love you, no more witty antics, no more lightning up a room with her smile, and no more moments of her being a mom to her 3 wonderful kid. The sadness and the reality of this being our life now is overwhelming. It's not fair!!

It all started on a beautiful evening on June 24, 2016 with her enjoying one of her favorite things, being on a boat. She was simply enjoying the summer night not knowing that a man under the influence who was driving too fast on that same river would take everything away in a split second. He never even saw the pontoon boat she was on and he killed her. He took her from us, her kids, her family, her many friends, and from her future. He took so much from us.

We will never be the same people we were before. We know we have many blessings with our other girls and our precious grandkids but no matter where we are or what we are doing, that dark cloud is right under the surface ready to show itself at any given minute.

Megan should be here, she should be enjoying her life. Her death was 100% avoidable. It was taken way too soon by an irresponsible person on that same river she enjoyed so much who was never held accountable for his actions. Thirty months probation for taking a life and so much more from so many people who Megan was so special to. JUSTICE?? We think not!!

So please, the next time you pick up a drink make sure you don't have plans to get behind the wheel of anything. It is not just the roadways. We were told because it happened on the river while boating it's not the same. Boating is more recreational than driving a car but when under the influence, the outcome is the same. A life was taken because of an intoxicated driver being irresponsible. I know Megan would be here today if this man hadn't made the decisions he made on June 24, 2016. He took a life and left so many people in heartbreaking pain. Lives were changed forever that day and now the world is missing a beautiful life.

An Afterword by Attorney Cindi Koroll

Subject: Megan

"We live in a system that espouses merit, equality, and a level playing field, but exalts those with wealth, power, and celebrity, however gained."
- Derrick Bell

Though I never met Megan Swaziek during her lifetime, I feel that I know her well. She has come alive to me through the love and remembrances of her family. Megan's mother, Robin Swaziek, fills her Facebook page with Megan's photos. In each, Megan is vibrant and alive. Her smile is beautiful often showing a hint of mischief and play. I would have liked Megan- even though she was a devout Packer's fan (Go Bears)!

On June 24, 2016, Dave and Robin Swaziek became members of a club no one wants to join "parents who have lost a child". However, Megan was not lost, she did not pass or go to a better place or any of the feeble platitudes we use when talking about death. Megan was taken. From her children, from her parents and sisters, from her life and her future.

On a beautiful day in June of 2016, Marc Mongan, Ogle County pharmacist and pharmacy owner took away the future of Megan Swaziek Wells. Megan was sitting in her favorite spot on her uncle's pontoon and looking forward to a June day on the river. Marc Mongan recklessly drove his jon boat (flat bottomed fishing boat) into and over the top of the back half of the idling pontoon hitting Megan, taking her off her seat and throwing her into the water. Megan Swaziek Wells, 31 years old, mother of three, died of blunt force trauma to her chest. A coroner's jury deemed Megan's death a homicide.

Homicide: the intentional and unlawful taking of another person's life. 720 ILCS 5/9-1 Statutory penalty. "Shall be sentenced" "Not less than 3 years-not more than 14 years.

625 ILCS 45/5 Operation of a Watercraft

Every person convicted of violating this Section shall be guilty of a Class 2 felony if the offense results in the death of a person. A person guilty of a Class 2 felony under this paragraph 5, if sentenced to a term of imprisonment, shall be sentenced to a term of not less than 3 years and not more than 14 years.

The Illinois Department of Natural Resources investigating police officer's report contains Mr. Mongan's admission to consuming 6 alcoholic drinks. Later Mongan would retract that admission and would reduce it to 2 drinks. Finally, at deposition Marc Mongan claimed that he had ordered a drink with his lunch but did not consume it. Credible? No.

Within minutes after Mongan crashed his boat into Megan, Mongan's entitlement and status in the community was evident. Mongan refused a request for blood alcohol testing.

The IDNR officer contacted the States Attorney seeking a warrant to determine the blood alcohol content of Mr. Mongan's blood. States Attorney Eric Morrow refused to get the warrant, "I know Marc Mongan, I know his family, he's not going anywhere." The response is outrageous. Marc Mongan was intoxicated. There was no doubt that Mongan drove into the pontoon. Megan was dead. Mongan refused all chemical tests. The facts required a warrant. The State's Attorney gave Mongan a gift. Privilege, prestige? He gave Megan disrespect, nonchalance.

Warrants are routinely obtained for chemical testing when a driver refuses. Specifically, if the driver in a crash fails a sobriety test, or as in Mongan's case admits to 6 drinks, smells like alcohol, and is staggering, and a death has occurred a warrant is within the policy and procedure of law enforcement in any case with a death. The issue of the phone call between the State's Attorney and the IDNR officer surfaced again, and the two parties met. In the conversation, the States Attorney asked the IDNR officials to "agree to disagree" that no warrant was sought. No such agreement was reached.

The refusal of the States Attorney's office to obtain a warrant for blood testing would be followed by a series of unfair, unjust, unethical, bizarre, and unexplainable events. Throughout it all Megan's family stood firm, present outside the Court house at every court date, decked out in red shirts, holding signs with Megan's picture and demanding justice.

What is justice? A grand jury was convened. The States Attorney selected the witnesses. and did not call any of the 3 people on the pontoon as witnesses. Why? Given the lack of testimony the grand jury refused to indict.

Soon after Megan's parents received a letter from the States Attorney claiming the sobriety testing was flawed and he intended to drop all charges. Reluctantly the States Attorney agreed to meet with Dave and Robin. Dave placed Megan's picture on the table. The attorney pushed the photo back at least twice. Did Megan's life matter?

Disillusioned and angry Megan's parents fought to maintain the case against Mongan ultimately turning to the office of the Attorney General. The AG suggested they should get a lawyer and file a Motion under the Crime Victims Act to become parties in the case.

As a nurse-attorney practicing in the area of personal injury, I was surprised by a call from David Swaziek (Swaz). He had received a referral to me from a counselor who described me as an aggressive and unrelenting advocate. I must agree also with that characterization, and I also acknowledge that in my advocacy I have overstepped my bounds and I am working on that. My passion for my cases can be excessive.

We filed the motion and Megan's parents were permitted to participate in the case. This gave them a voice- though limited. We filed our first motion to disqualify the States Attorney and to Obtain a Special Prosecutor. We lost the hard-fought motion as the State vehemently asserted no conflict existed. A week later, the State's Attorney called us in to advise that they were filing a motion agreeing to a Special Prosecutor as due to the appearance of impropriety. When their motion was brought before the Court, Judge Reddington repeatedly asked Counsel whether there was or was or was not a conflict. Unsatisfied with the answers received the Judge stated, "Counsel, no one is a little bit pregnant."

Megan's family was excited! Armed with a Special Prosecutor who did not have community ties, justice for Megan might be possible. With the Special Prosecutor, in short order came a new grand jury and a seven-count felony indictment. Sadly a "deal "was made allowing Mongan to plead to only one felony count and dismissal of the other 6 felonies. Mongan was sentenced to probation, community service, a short restriction on alcohol use and boating. This is NOT "Justice for Megan".

Mongan added insult to injury when, in response to the sincere and moving victim impact statements from Megan's family. Marc Mongan stood and apologized to his wife and daughters for the disruption in their lives, he said nothing to Megan's grieving family.

Other than his status as a convicted felon, Marc Mongan's life has not changed much. He continues to have an active license to practice as a pharmacist and can still operate his pharmacy business. The licensing board has stated that because the felony conviction was not related to his practice of pharmacy, he can retain his license. However, we are not finished with that aspect of his case. Please note licenses can be suspended for a failure to pay income tax. A felony involving alcohol and a death is a higher offense than a failure to pay taxes.

While Mongan's life has not changed and our efforts to obtain justice for Megan have not changed, I am forever changed. Trying to get Justice for Megan has been the most meaningful, significant case in my career. Megan's family has graced me with the title of Megan's Angel. They have invited me to their home for dinner, included me in Megan's birthday celebrations. They are good people. This never should have happened to them.

Depriving criminals of their freedom is a deterrent to future crimes. As a criminal sanctioning option, jails provide a method of holding offenders accountable for criminal acts. At deposition, Marc Mongan argued against the label of "felon". But Marc Mongan *IS* a felon. If the powers that be had their way he would have walked away, without even so much as a traffic ticket.

As to Justice for Megan? Our efforts continue. Megan's life mattered.

Cindi Koroll, RN, JD

GALLERY

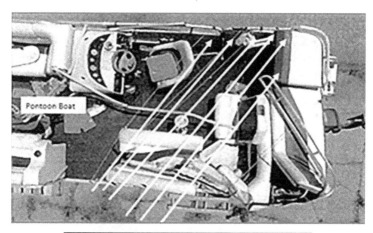

Pontoon boat Megan
Was on sitting in the
back

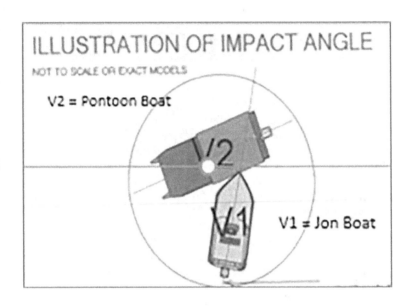

ILLUSTRATION OF IMPACT ANGLE

NOT TO SCALE OR EXACT MODELS

V2 = Pontoon Boat

V1 = Jon Boat

Jon Boat

CPSIA information can be obtained
at www.ICGtesting.com
Printed in the USA
BVHW042127100122
625960BV00013B/918